Sydney Anglicanism

Sydney Anglicanism

An Apology

Michael P. Jensen

WIPF & STOCK · Eugene, Oregon

SYDNEY ANGLICANISM
An Apology

Copyright © 2012 Michael P. Jensen. All rights reserved. Except for brief quotations in critical publications or reviews, no part of this book may be reproduced in any manner without prior written permission from the publisher. Write: Permissions, Wipf and Stock Publishers, 199 W. 8th Ave., Suite 3, Eugene, OR 97401.

Wipf & Stock
An Imprint of Wipf and Stock Publishers
199 W. 8th Ave., Suite 3
Eugene, OR 97401
www.wipfandstock.com

ISBN 13: 978-1-61097-465-3
Manufactured in the U.S.A.

All scripture quotations, unless otherwise indicated, are taken from the Holy Bible, New International Version®, NIV®. Copyright ©1973, 1978, 1984 by Biblica, Inc.™ Used by permission of Zondervan. All rights reserved worldwide.

*To the archbishops of Sydney
past and present*

Contents

1 Introduction / 1

Part One: The Bible

2 Are Sydney Anglicans Fundamentalists? / 13
3 What the Bible Means: The Significance of "Biblical Theology" / 30
4 Propositional Revelation the Only Revelation? Scripture and Revelation in the Diocese of Sydney / 43
5 The Romance of Preaching and the Sydney Sermon / 57

Part Two: The Church

6 "Wherever Two or Three Are Gathered": The Knox-Robinson Doctrine of the Church / 75
7 Are Sydney Anglicans Actually Anglicans? / 90
8 The Church and the World / 109
9 Sydney Anglicans and the Ministry of Women / 126
10 The Great Cause? The Push for Lay Administration at the Lord's Supper / 144
11 Church Politics and the Anglican Church League / 160
12 Conclusion / 173
    Bibliography / 177
    Index / 181

one

Introduction

Indomitable Sydney?

The famous *Asterix the Gaul* comic books that I read when I was a kid begin in this way:

> The year is 50 B.C. Gaul is entirely occupied by the Romans. Well, not entirely... One small village of indomitable Gauls still holds out against the invaders. And life is not easy for the Roman legionaries who garrison the fortified camps of Totorum, Aquarium, Laudanum and Compendium...[1]

The Gauls gain their fabulous strength from a magic potion brewed by their druid, Getafix. But the secret of their ability to defy the odds, and the Romans, comes from somewhere else. They are possessed of a remarkable inner fortitude. They have an almost casual confidence about them that drives their opponents to distraction. They have a clear sense of shared identity in the face of what seems like insurmountable opposition. They love to eat wild boar.

The way the story of the Anglican diocese of Sydney has been told by her supporters and critics alike often sounds like the opening to *Asterix*. In the view of Melbourne journalist and Anglican laywoman Muriel Porter, for example, the evangelical variety of Anglicanism that in general characterizes the diocese of Sydney is defiantly peculiar.[2]

---

1. Goscinny and Uderzo, *Asterix the Gaul*, 3.
2. Porter's distaste has been most lately expressed in Porter, *Sydney Anglicans*.

Sydney Anglicanism

As she reads it, an Anglicanism that is Catholic in liturgy and liberal in theology has triumphed everywhere. It is the dominant form, and reigns unchecked and unchallenged across Australia and even across the globe. This one small diocese of indomitable, very conservative, and (to be frank) completely unhinged evangelical Anglicans holds out against the onward march of liberal Catholic Anglicanism. And life is, as a result, not easy for those who surround it and have to deal with it. Sydney's commitment to lay presidency at the Lord's Supper[3] and its objection to the ordination of women to the priesthood are symptoms of the baffling and stubborn irrationality that characterizes the diocese. They simply get in the way of what would be a normal development in other places.

The same story can be told from within the gates of the Sydney Anglican village as well. While all around, Anglicanism has capitulated almost totally to the liberal, broad-church paradigm—with the exception a few parishes in each diocese that are allowed to remain traditional Anglo-Catholic or conservative evangelical—Sydney is the only diocese in which an evangelical form of Anglicanism holds sway. Alone it holds the torch against the onslaught of darkness. Alone it defies the complete capitulation of Anglican Christianity to Western cultural mores. Alone it holds to priority of Scripture over culture as authoritative for church belief and practice. Splendidly, nobly alone.

It is the thesis of this book that this narrative is simply untrue and that holding to it is potentially disastrous. From both perspectives, the story has its undoubted appeal. For the critic, it is a means to write off Sydney's form of Anglicanism as extremist. It is so weird, so manifestly eccentric, that it must be maintained by a powerful cadre of warriors who drink from a magic potion. Critics like to emphasize the words "powerful" and "hardline" with reference to Sydney diocese, because strong-arm tactics are surely the only way this bizarre twist on Anglican faith could be upheld. For the supporter, there is something compelling about belonging to a group that is so savagely attacked by its critics. The sense of a shared identity as we collectively hold against the terrible odds is worth the cost of the nastiness directed against us. Indeed, the

---

3. "Lay presidency" is the practice of allowing an unordained person to lead the congregation in the service of Holy Communion—usually reserved for the minister ordained as priest in Anglican churches.

more the critic spits his poisonous words, the more we draw a collective energy from the shared experience of being talked about in such a way.

But however appealing it is, the story is distinctly inaccurate. To be fair, the diocese of Sydney has a unique character as a predominantly evangelical metropolitan diocese in Australia.[4] But it shares its evangelical convictions with many millions of Anglicans all over the world in continuity with those in the past. In fact, as far as worldwide Anglicanism goes, it is evangelicalism that is on the rise. Liberal-Catholic Anglicans, on the other hand, are good at inhabiting church structures, but not good at missionary work—nor even at the business of catechizing their own young people. Evangelical Anglicans of the sort found in Sydney have good ground for claiming the Anglican heritage as their own and ought not to accept the view that they are in some way the illegitimate children of the Anglican family. Sydney is not, as I hope to show, as isolated and eccentric as its critics pretend.

Their critics have dubious grounds for holding to the *Asterix* narrative, and Sydney's Anglicans shouldn't fall for its allure either. It is dangerous to tell such stories about oneself, because isolationism is ultimately unhealthy. Taking too much notice of one's critics makes clear-eyed self-awareness all the more difficult. Friendly criticism is too readily cast as betrayal. It is too simple to cast one's identity in terms of difference and to see the purpose of one's existence in negative rather than positive terms. This is, as I shall argue, exactly what the critics of Sydney want: to isolate it further so it can be treated as completely marginal.

But there is far more to the diocese of Sydney than this. It is not a fundamentalist sect. It has a rich and developing heritage of robust and intellectually vigorous evangelical faith. It aspires to be a genuinely missionary movement, concerned to send people to all corners of the globe and to contribute to the spread of the Christian faith everywhere. It is not marginal or eccentric, unless staking oneself on the authority of Scripture has somehow become marginal and eccentric in Christianity. It is conservative on content and flexible on form—which is surely the way in which historic Christianity has, under the hand of God, been preserved and expanded over two millennia.

---

4. The Anglican Church of Australia is, granted, almost unique amongst Anglican churches in that the dioceses have a great independence over against the national church. See Kaye, *A Church without Walls*, 112.

Wrestling the Leviathan

It surprises visitors to Sydney to learn what a brutal and bruising place it can be. The playwright David Williamson described it once as the "Emerald City"—an image that captured the extraordinary sensuality and prosperity of the shimmering city but also the Gollumish greed that it nurses. Sydney is desperate to please and desperate to be pleased; the local band The Whitlams once sang of it as "a whore / opening its legs to the world." It looks like it is going to be an easy place to live, until you discover that the citizens of Sydney are clambering over each other's prone bodies just to stake their claim for a harbor view. It looks as if Sydney is all about desire and especially about sex—it has an entire festival, the Gay and Lesbian Mardi Gras dedicated to sexuality. In reality her addictions are work—and power.

It is a civilization founded on the sound of the lash, the burning taste of rum and the sweat of the chain gang. Things have gotten a lot better for the locals since those days, but those early lessons haven't been forgotten. You have to be tough to survive here, even as a clergyman. When local journalist John Birmingham wrote a book about the monstrous side of Sydney's character he called it after the biblical sea monster: *Leviathan*.[5] It's a great description of Sydney. She's a sea-beast wearing mascara; a snake showing a bit of leg. She has a come-hither gaze and a murky heart.

Sydney lacks the urbanity and cultural pretentions of little sister Melbourne. The culture of its political parties is more pragmatic and less ideological. The NSW branch of the Australian Labor Party, for example, is dominated by its famous Right faction. It would be a mistake to say that the Labor Right is without ideals. It is just that, in Sydney, the beauty of the ends is not felt to be corrupted by the ugliness of the means. It has no interest in flavorless virtues like "balance."

That same difference of culture can been observed in church circles. It has been noted regularly, to the point of cliché, but it is certainly not inaccurate. The person who chooses to be a god-botherer amongst the descendants of convicts and gold-diggers is not usually a person who is afraid of being out of kilter with the prevailing culture. The Sydney Anglican subculture is therefore built on a one-eyed determination to survive—because the expectation is that no one else is

---

5. Birmingham, *Leviathan*.

going to cut you any slack. Ministering in the early colony broke the spirit of Rev. Richard Johnson, the first chaplain. He was replaced by the somewhat sturdier figure of Rev. Samuel Marsden—the Yorkshireman now legendary in Sydney history as "the flogging parson," since he acted as magistrate as well as pastor to the colony and (according to the myth) was not averse to meting out severe discipline. But he was also generous of spirit and keen to see the gospel of Jesus proclaimed in the unchartered territories of the south, including New Zealand as well as Australia.

The first chaplains of the colony of New South Wales were evangelical churchmen. They left a permanent impress on the type of Anglicanism that would be found in Sydney. By the late eighteenth century, the evangelical movement within the Church of England was on the rise. What it lacked in ecclesiastical preferment, it made up for in entrepreneurial spirit and missionary zeal. It was no accident that the first clergy to arrive were recruited from among the ranks of the evangelicals. The movement would reach its high point sometime in the 1830s, when the Oxford Movement began the revival of the High Church party within Anglicanism. In Sydney, however, the presence of a growing number of Irish Roman Catholics meant that there was a need on the Anglican side for clergy who would understand what was at stake. Many early Sydney clergy were recruited from the Church of Ireland, where a clear Protestant identity was necessary for survival.

The problem of recruiting and training clergy was always a pressing one. When the bequest of Thomas Moore (1762–1840), a wealthy shipbuilder and landowner, was made available for the "education of men of the Protestant persuasion," Bishop Barker (1808–1882) arranged for the founding of Moore College. The college opened its doors for students at Liverpool in 1856, and moved to its present site in Newtown in 1891. To this day, Moore College is central to the identity of the Sydney diocese. Unlike in the Church of England, where a diocese may employ clergy trained at any number of different colleges, in Sydney local clergy are trained at Moore, with a very few exceptions.

It's a policy that has often been questioned, but it is key to maintaining the evangelical character of the diocese. The Anglicanism of compromise and nominalism lives by the power of inertia. It rises to the top in so many places around the world because it isn't challenged. Over a century and half, evangelicals in Sydney have been determined that a different character would mark their diocese. That has meant an, at times, angular relationship with a national church in which many other agendas are running.

This background goes some way in explaining why the diocese of Sydney has been the subject of a number of books and articles over the last two decades, including a book published in 2011—Muriel Porter's *Sydney Anglicans and the Threat to World Anglicanism*.[6] No one has written in this way about, say, Melbourne diocese or even the diocese of London. Needless to say, none of these works is appreciative and some are scathing. And, from my point of view as an insider, none of these books does justice to the object of their derision.

An Apology?

My vantage point is a great deal different. I grew up at Moore College, one of the ventricles of the Anglican diocese of Sydney. My father, the present Archbishop of Sydney, was the principal of that college. In my early years of high school it became clear to me that there were other Anglicans who were very critical of Moore and of the diocese of Sydney. The denomination in which I found my home was actively and openly hostile to the kind of Anglican I had learned to be. They called the church that I attended "not really Anglican." But if it wasn't "really Anglican" then what was it?

Since I have been old enough to read newspapers or to care what they had to say, the *Sydney Morning Herald* has run a narrative about Sydney Anglicans, siding very much with the views of those liberal Anglican critics. Since the early 1980s, I can recall reading very few articles about church life that I recognized to be accurate or fair to my experience of it. The depiction was always of a rabidly fundamentalist patriarchal sect doggedly hanging on to its outmoded views against all comers, and for the sheer heck of it. The favorite adjective was "powerful," with all the overtones of menace and skullduggery.

I have called this book *Sydney Anglicanism: An Apology*, and I need to be clear about what I mean by this. In the first place, "Sydney Anglicanism" is a technically inaccurate designation. There are Anglicans in the Sydney diocese, such as those at the parishes of St. James,' King

---

6. Porter, *Sydney Anglicans*.

Introduction

St. and Christ Church, St. Laurence and at several others, who have a valued and historic place in the life of the diocese but who express a very different kind of Anglicanism to the sort known as "Sydney Anglicanism." It is with some apology to them that I use the term to describe the Reformed and evangelical flavor of the Christianity for which the diocese has become widely known. Secondly, there are many evangelical Anglicans in Australia and around the world who would share the outlook of "Sydney" Anglicans. It is slightly misleading to use the "Sydney" label as if the evangelicalism of Sydney is only found there.

But why "An Apology"? This book could easily be the mirror image of the kind of criticism that has been leveled at Sydney. It could be a one-eyed defense on all counts against all charges. But that kind of apology falls for a terrible trap. It accepts the terms set for it by its critics and also accepts the standard of truth set by them. The reality is that the Sydney diocese is nothing like the monstrosity that its detractors think it has become, but also is not an idealized New Jerusalem of evangelicalism either. The best kind of apology will also contain elements of honest critique.

I cannot pretend to simple objectivity. Not at all. This is a book written from the heart of its subject. I am an eyewitness to some of the events I describe. I am a friend, relative, and colleague of some of the protagonists. Presently, I teach doctrine and church history at Moore College. Nevertheless, in what follows I hope to surmount the old pattern of tirade and counter-tirade. I do think that Sydney's form of Anglicanism is remarkable, and that it is (under God) in the possession of the heritage and resources to make it a powerful witness for Christ in the Australia of the twenty-first century.[7]

The book falls into two sections: "The Bible" and "The Church." The distinctive contributions that Sydney Anglicans have made relate to these areas. They are conservative, orthodox Protestant Christians, but it would be wrong to label them fundamentalists (chapter 2). They have developed a particular way of reading Scripture that is intellectually and spiritually robust (chapter 3). They hold that God has revealed himself in words (chapter 4). They preach from Scripture in a particular way and are known for the kind of sermons they preach (chapter 5).

---

7. A potential limitation on my perspective is that I have never been a member of any Anglican synod, whether at local or national level.

In the area of the church, Sydney's Anglicans have some striking things to say but also some serious challenges to meet. This is the sphere of many of the controversies of the present era. They have developed a particular doctrine of the church, with an emphasis on the local gathering (chapter 6). They have a genuine claim to the heritage of Anglicanism but also need to decide what that means for the future (chapter 7). They have not always successfully managed their relationship to "the world" outside the church (chapter 8). The controversy about the ordination of women has perhaps been the defining moment for Sydney Anglicans and has brought much opprobrium their way (chapter 9). The push of lay administration at the Lord's Supper has likewise brought the differences between Sydney diocese and other forms of Anglicans into sharp focus but not always to a great result (chapter 10). Sydney has been known for its ability to manage it political processes to an evangelical outcome (chapter 11).

Above all, I am convinced that the best way to read "Sydney Anglicanism," whether to laud it or lionize it, is as human phenomena. Whatever it is, it is neither more sinister nor more glorious than anything else that human beings do collectively. Where it is admirable, it is because it is faithful to God. Where it is less so, it is because it is scared by the limitations and sins of its adherents—their insecurities, their pride, their mistakes, and blind spots. It would be a mistake to boast in it without also acknowledging its flaws. But the Christian conviction is that the Father of Jesus Christ chooses to work in and with his people, by his Spirit, and not aside from them—and to him be the glory.

This book was written mainly in a flurry of energy that came to me somewhat mysteriously in a ten-week period at the end of 2010. Since then, the labor has been more heavy-going, and I have had to rely on the assistance and advice of friends and colleagues. Dr Peter Bolt deserves particular mention. His careful reading of the manuscript saved me from many embarrassing errors and forced me to consider more carefully what I had written at many points. Stephen Gardner and Andrew Judd were willing research assistants, tracking down unsourced quotations and forgotten page references, and serving as critical first readers. Drs. David Höhne and Greg Anderson heard the contents of the book repeatedly on our morning runs and provided insight and advice. Nick Davies, Luke Collings, and Marty Kemp offered astute comments on a late draft. The governing board of Moore College has provided funds towards the completion of the book and I thank them. While I cannot take credit for all the things that are right about this book, I certainly do bear the burden of any mistakes.

Part One:

The Bible

two

Are Sydney Anglicans Fundamentalists?

A Disagreeable Word

"Fundamentalism" is a disagreeable word; and someone who is a fundamentalist is usually thought to be a disagreeable person. It is a label that has been frequently applied to Sydney Anglicans. Because of their stubborn conviction on the authority of Scripture, there's no doubt that Sydney Anglicans are, theologically speaking, very conservative. They are anti-progressive in the sense that, for them, the word of God "stands written"; there is no further substantive revelation, nor any virtue in "moving on" from Scripture. It is a good deposit to be guarded, the "faith once delivered to all the saints" (Jude 1:3). Sydney Anglicans also regard themselves as ambivalent about modernity. But it would be a mistake to call them "fundamentalists" in the modern sense. They often are so called by their detractors, but the term of abuse is inaccurate and unfair.

"Fundamentalist" is a playground bully among words. It is a word hissed through clenched teeth. It could be argued on this account that it isn't worth taking the concept of fundamentalism seriously, because it usually means "a religious person who is more conservative than me, and in an irritating way." But there *is* such a thing as fundamentalism. It is a real phenomenon, and Sydney Anglicans need to be clear to themselves and to others about why they don't share in it.

There *are* contemporary Christians who would proudly call themselves "fundamentalists," living chiefly in the US. Contemporary

Sydney Anglicanism

Christian fundamentalism is distinguished by (though not defined by) teachings like six-day creationism, pre-millennial eschatology, and a particularly right-wing approach to politics.[1] None of these things are characteristic of Sydney Anglicans.[2] Like millions of other Christians, they trace their heritage to mainstream and orthodox theologians like John Calvin and Martin Luther, who upheld the supreme authority of Scripture in the church. Holding to the supreme authority of Scripture does not in itself make you a "fundamentalist," however irritating this is to Christians who differ. What it does mean is that, as they see it, tradition, reason, and experience will never trump Scripture as an authority.

The original "fundamentalists" were a broad movement that began in response to theological modernism. A wealthy American businessman named Lyman Stewart (1840–1923) commissioned and funded a group of writers to write a series of defensive books and tracts that were to be labeled "The Fundamentals." These tracts appeared in great numbers between 1912 and 1916. Some of the tracts were by scholars of note; others were not quite so impressive. The word "fundamentalist"

---

1. See Noll, *The Scandal of the Evangelical Mind*.

2. It is worth noting that the 2006 National Church Life Survey frequencies for the following question for Sydney Anglicans were as follows:

Which statement best represents your view of the Bible? (Mark ONE only)

a. *The Bible is the word of God, to be taken literally word for word*

b. *The Bible is the word of God to be interpreted in the light of its historical and cultural context*

c. *The Bible is the word of God, to be interpreted in the light of the Church's teaching and traditions*

d. *The Bible is not the word of God but a unique book through which God's word may come to us*

e. *The Bible is not the word of God but is a valuable book*

f. *The Bible is an ancient book with little value today*

g. *Don't know*

a. 25.6%
b. 50.8%
c. 20.5%
d. 2.6%
e. 0
f. 0
g. 0.5%

The majority of Sydney Anglican pew-sitters clearly identify their view of Scripture in line with what we might call a classical Protestant understanding—nearly twice as many who would identify with the broadly fundamentalist view, and considerably more than would own the more "catholic" view. If Sydney Anglicans are notorious fundamentalists, then why isn't this reflected in the statistical data?

however was the lasting label given to the conservative form of Christianity that it represented—especially as it was determined to defend Christianity from radical modernism in theology and culture. Quickly, the fundamentalists lost credibility and their reputation became tarnished. They seemed ignorant: of the issues they were addressing, of the Bible they were defending, and especially of science. They became more zealous; and they were despised. They came from, and appealed to, the less educated parts of the Christian world.

Things happen a little more slowly in Australia. In a piece originally published in 1987 entitled "What Shall We Do With The Bible?" Archbishop Donald Robinson (1922-) recounted his own experience of the shift in the usage of the term.[3] When he went to Sydney University in 1940, he was not unhappy to own the label "fundamentalist." It merely indicated then that he was not a modernist and was committed to the authority of Scripture. As the term increasingly was being used by the opponents of evangelicals to caricature and abuse them, prominent evangelicals began to disavow it from the 1950s on—especially in the UK. Leading British evangelical Anglican John Stott (1922–2011) was in the vanguard. As Robinson writes:

> He said we ought to discard it [the term fundamentalist] because it had become associated with three extravagances, first, a total rejection of all biblical criticism, secondly, excessively literalist interpretation of the Bible and thirdly, certain rather mechanical theories of the nature of biblical inspiration. Those extravagances, he said, were no part of the orthodox evangelical position or of the IVF in particular.[4]

Another leading British evangelical J. I. Packer (1926-) likewise detested the term as a description for evangelicalism, and authored a book called *"Fundamentalism" and the Word of God*—with the quotation marks in the title indicating that he thought that the word was not something he could now own.

It was clearly a word that made evangelicals wince, and so their opponents continued to use it. And evangelicals continued to seek to distinguish themselves from it. An American evangelical scholar named E. J. Carnell (1919–1967) argued that fundamentalism had become more

---

3. Robinson, *Donald Robinson*, 2:24–28.
4. Ibid., 27. The "IVF" is the "InterVarsity Fellowship," the leading evangelical student movement.

of a religious attitude than a theological position.[5] Fundamentalists claimed to sit under Scripture's authority, but in fact they followed their own traditions and habits in interpreting the Bible. They had failed to develop an affirmative worldview and would not try to connect their convictions with the culture. Their only goal was to negate modernism. But once modernism itself had died away, fundamentalism had no obvious *raison d'etre*. It became a highly rigid and ideologically driven form of Christianity, incapable of recognizing incompleteness and inconsistency in its own position or of tolerating it in anyone else. As Carnell wrote:

> Fundamentalism is a lonely position. It has cut itself off from the general stream of culture, philosophy and ecclesiastical tradition. This accounts, in part, for its robust pride. Since it is no longer in union with the wisdom of the ages, it has no standard by which to judge its own religious pretense."[6]

This characterization of fundamentalism as a mentality rather than a particular position was taken up by the British biblical scholar James Barr (1924–2006) in his 1977 book *Fundamentalism*,[7] in which he offered a sweeping critique of the evangelical InterVarsity Press and its publications. Barr's chief target in his book was the evangelicalism of the British scene. Yet the British evangelicals had always been adamant that they were *not* fundamentalists and that they held none of the tenets of fundamentalism as it was found in the US: they were not young earth creationists, they were not pre-millennialist, they were not prone to the worst excesses of the holiness movement, and so on. For Barr, these things were beside the point. The specifics of dogma were irrelevant. What counted was the defensive mentality.

Donald Robinson is aware of Barr's critique and is at pains to show how his evangelical commitment to the authority of Scripture does not operate as a mere "religious mentality." He concedes that some evangelicals are indeed guilty of the kind of attitudes decried by Carnell and Barr. But being committed to the authority of Scripture ought to result in a theological method that is not subject to the charge laid against fundamentalism, not at all. Robinson wrote:

---

5. Carnell's position is described by Robinson, *Donald Robinson*, 2:29.
6. Carnell, *The Case for Orthodox Theology*, 113–26.
7. Barr, *Fundamentalism*.

> The first task of theology as I see it is the understanding of the revelation of the Scriptures in their own original terms, that is, in the language and cultural forms in which it was originally given. The second task is to express and interpret that understanding in relation to the language and cultural forms of our own day and in response to questions and concerns which arise from our own life, some of which did not arise in the life of Bible times. Yet even the disciplined theological task which I have described is not a static or isolated one. It does not take place in a vacuum. There is and always has been the continuous fellowship of the people of God, the actual living of the life of faith by individuals and churches, the preaching of the gospel and the exercise of various spiritual ministries.[8]

For Robinson, the practice of the authority of Scripture ought to result in a rigorous biblical scholarship and attentiveness to contemporary questions and concerns. And it ought to take place in conversation with and with respect to the venerable tradition of Christian—and not necessarily just evangelical—interpretation of the Bible.

In outlining this method and in exemplifying it in his work over four decades as a churchman and a scholar, Robinson bequeathed to Sydney Anglicans the possibility of an intellectually robust evangelicalism. He showed that a Reformation conviction on the supreme authority of Scripture need not be at odds with scholarly integrity, nor need it result in the kind of defensive obscurantism displayed in fundamentalism. To this day, the students at Moore College, who have access to the best and most comprehensive theological library in the southern hemisphere, are encouraged to read and to learn from the works of scholars from a variety of traditions and not just those that agree with them. And yet, this has not prevented the critics of Sydney Anglicanism from applying the term to them. It is to the work of one of those critics that we now turn.

Muriel Porter's The New Puritans

Donald Robinson's attempt to distinguish Sydney Anglicanism from fundamentalism is not enough for Sydney's critics, who continue to use the term as a pejorative. One such recent example is Muriel Porter's

---

8. Robinson, *Donald Robinson*, 2:30.

book *The New Puritans: The Rise of Fundamentalism in the Anglican Church*.[9] Make no mistake: Porter loathes Sydney Anglicanism and is not afraid to say so. This book is a piece of polemic rather than having any pretense to some kind of scholarly objectivity (as the author herself admits). The title of her project is an indication of her purpose. If she can prove that Sydney Anglicans are rightly labeled "fundamentalists" then that is, in a sense, enough. In the minds of the audience to which Porter imagines she is writing, fundamentalism is *per definition* a very bad thing. Her thesis is that the "Sydney Diocese is now in several key respects fundamentalist although it detests this badge";[10] therefore, she denies the right of Sydney Anglicans to self-describe. In fact, protesting against being called "fundamentalists" (as Robinson has done) is exactly what fundamentalists do.

She is right that Sydney Anglicans do not wish to be called fundamentalists. Robinson's successor as archbishop, Peter Jensen (1943–), sought to distinguish fundamentalism from his kind of evangelicalism in his first major address following his election in 2001. In that speech he outlined fundamentalism as implying "an anti-intellectual, backward-looking and ugly zeal in the cause of religion."[11] He agrees that both the fundamentalist and the evangelical hold to the supreme authority of Scripture. The difference is that, while the evangelical interprets the Bible "literally," the fundamentalist interprets it "literalistically." A literal or plain reading of Scripture might still make use of traditional interpretation, the genuine advances of modern biblical scholarship, and opens itself to learning from contemporary thought. The literalistic reading does not.

Porter is less than impressed by this speech and doesn't acknowledge the difference between "literal" and "literalistic."[12] There is more to fundamentalism than that, she says, and points to James Barr's notion of the particular "fundamentalist mentality."[13] What is that mentality?

---

9. Porter, *The New Puritans*.

10. Ibid., 22.

11. Jensen, "Presidential Address."

12. One of the difficulties with the term "literal" is that in common usage it has come to mean "literalistic." In the Reformation, it merely indicated a repudiation of allegorical readings of texts. At least in part through its association with fundamentalism, the term "literal" has acquired the more degraded meaning.

13. Peter Jensen actually acknowledged a similar kind of definition in his speech.

Are Sydney Anglicans Fundamentalists?

Porter wheels on the definitions provided by Oxford academic Harriet Harris: a rationalist mindset, a "Calvinistic zeal to root out error and preserve doctrinal purity," charismatic and authoritarian leadership, behavioral requirements, and a tendency to separatism. This list is of course not arbitrary. Porter's determination is to define "fundamentalism" in such a way that her description of Sydney Anglicanism fits the definition. But the definition is already decided by her perceptions of Sydney Anglicans. While she acknowledges that there is a vast literature in the study of religion about fundamentalism, she overlooks that and chooses the one study that suits her polemical purposes best.[14] Sydney Anglicanism is fundamentalist because fundamentalism is whatever Sydney Anglicans are.

But even so, Porter's critique fails to convince. First, she claims that Sydney is "rationalistic." Porter claims that the Sydney commitment to "propositional revelation" is evidence of this self-evidently egregious rationalism—that is of course evidence of fundamentalism, on the terms she has decided beforehand:

> The theory [i.e. propositional revelation] refers to revelation imparted through rational thought processes alone, without any subsidiary, complementary or external revelatory processes, such as through sensuous experiences mediated through liturgy, music, nature or Eucharistic participation.

Certainly, the emphasis on the Bible as revelation is the Sydney emphasis, and she is right to say that Sydney Anglican church services stress the reading, hearing, and preaching of the word of God over against other aspects. But it is not accurate to describe this in terms of "rational thought processes." It is the hearing of the word, which has personal and existential and emotional and experiential impact—as Luther said, "the ears are the organ of the Christian." Faith comes from hearing, after all (Rom 10:17). It seems uncontroversial to uphold, in a Protestant denomination, the verbal nature of the word of God (for that is all that is meant by 'propositional" revelation).[15]

Again, Porter rightly observes that what is at stake is a different view of how Scripture is meant to work. This is a crucial and revealing moment, for Porter at this point puts forward her version of the

---

14. Porter, *The New Puritans*, 23–24.
15. I will discuss this notion of propositional revelation in chapter 4.

Christian doctrine of revelation. What Porter wants is for the Holy Spirit to speak *outside of* Scripture so that her particular causes, especially the ordination of women to the priesthood and to the episcopacy, may be endorsed. She appeals to a vague sense of an extra-scriptural guidance that is not at the same time subject to the authority of Scripture. And she makes an attack on the classic Protestant doctrine of the clarity of Scripture—that now becomes another feature of fundamentalism (not before listed): "This support for a 'plain' meaning is a hallmark of the fundamentalist approach to Scripture."[16] However, the clarity of Scripture is a building block of the Reformation Christianity of the sixteenth century—the form of Christianity on which her own denomination is founded.

Then follows this paragraph:

> Many commentators have demonstrated that no "plain" reading is possible, given the nature of the Hebrew and Christian Scriptures, which are thousands of years old. They reflect entirely different thought-worlds from that of the twenty-first century, and are inevitably imbued with the ancient cultural patterns, norms and expectations from which they were written. More than a hundred years of scholarly criticism has revealed the complexity of interpreting the meaning of the Bible for contemporary Christians. Similarly, many scholars have pointed out clear examples of the Christian Church changing its mind as over the centuries it has read the Scriptures with fresh insight.

Porter names no such commentators or scholars or critics, despite citing them as indisputable authorities. Despite Donald Robinson's and Peter Jensen's protestation that Sydney Anglicans are in fact open to the genuine findings of contemporary biblical scholarship, Porter is insistent that this is not the case. She does not acknowledge the academic qualifications and publications—from secular universities and in leading research journals—of the biblical scholars from Moore.

Porter misrepresents the notion of the "plain" reading. Protestant interpreters have always acknowledged that the interpretation of Scripture is complex (as 2 Peter 3:16 tells us), and that new light may be shed on the meaning of the text. The notion of the plain reading of Scripture is in the first instance a commitment to read Scripture as a properly literary document and not to bring fanciful spiritual allegories to bear

---

16. Porter, *The New Puritans*, 26.

upon it. There seems to be a confusion here: on the one hand Porter wants to be able to say that the Holy Spirit can overrule the teachings of Scripture, but on the other she wants to say that reading the Scriptures with fresh insight matters. Why would fresh insight into Scripture matter if you weren't actually committed to the authority of Scripture? The example of slavery is brought out as a case in which people changed their minds about Scripture. This is, of course, not news. It was people who held to a doctrine of revelation like that of Sydney, such as the great reformer William Wilberforce, who decided that obedience to Scripture necessitated an end to slavery. He won because his reading of Scripture was in the end more convincing and more morally compelling than those who argued *for* slavery from Scripture. The danger with Porter's model of divine revelation, which seems to invite consideration of which social trends are the work of the Holy Spirit and which aren't, is that this logic could be used to support almost any cause you could name. How could Porter speak against an aberrant but widely-held development in society? This is where Porter's own extremism slips into view: she represents the extreme liberal wing of the Anglican Communion, in which the only authorities to which anyone is subject are gut feeling and the zeitgeist. Is "emotionalism" preferable to "rationalism"? Whatever the case, even if "rationalism" is a hallmark of fundamentalism, and even if the kind of rationalism that is meant by that term is found in Sydney, Porter has wandered far from this point and strayed into a discussion of the role and practice of the authority of Scripture. It is hard to see how it supports the point she is making.

As for the "zeal to root out error and doctrinal impurity," Porter resorts to an unfortunate sweeping gesture—"too many to discuss in detail here."[17] The somewhat trivial example that she *does* cite is the ban on the Anglo-Catholic use of the chasuble, which has been in force since 1910. Remembering that Porter is trying to show that the Sydney diocese has only become "fundamentalist" since 2001, this example is particularly strange. Other Anglican dioceses make requirements of their clergy vis-a-vis liturgical garments. Her second example is a piece of unsubstantiated hearsay: "refusal by many Sydney clergy to allow lay women to play any significant part in the main Sunday services— even reading lessons from the Bible—as a means of keeping faith with their claim that women must not exercise any leadership in mixed . . .

17. Ibid., 28.

congregations."[18] Not one concrete instance is cited. I personally travel to many different parishes in Sydney and I can say categorically that Porter is plainly wrong at this point. Lay and clergy women lead services, read lessons, lead in prayers, lead singing, and in some parishes preach. In my own parish, there are a number of women who serve in this way. Once again: the experience of evangelical clergy and candidates who hold a complementarian[19] view in other dioceses is that the authorities will insist on their alternative view with zeal and enforce it against others if necessary. Is this not "zeal to root out error and doctrinal impurity"?

The third point on her checklist is "charismatic and authoritarian leadership." In her sketch of the role of Sydney's archbishop, she provides a less than convincing case, noting that Sydney is historically committed to the priority of the parish. Parish clergy enjoy remarkable independence in Sydney, in fact, compared with other dioceses. While noting Peter Jensen's high profile, she admits "whether this equates with authoritarianism I do not know, but I suspect that this archbishop does not need to be authoritarian."[20] Is this not a concession that her argument is not established? Noting that there has been in Sydney a high degree of unity in the synod and so on is not exactly tantamount to establishing an authoritarian pattern. Again, it is worth observing that there are charismatic and authoritarian leaders in non-evangelical dioceses—indeed far more authoritarian than in Sydney. Archbishop Peter Carnley of Perth (1937–), well known for his liberal Catholic or "progressive Orthodox" views, was by all accounts just such a figure.

What of the last two points? As to behavioral requirements, Porter argues that Sydney has a "harsher set of rules concerning personal morality."[21] As evidence, she cites Sydney's policy on divorce and remarriage—though without giving specific details as to what it might be. Sydney's practice with regards to remarriage of divorced persons and divorced clergy is certainly less flexible than the free-for-all operating in some places in Australia. It remains, however, a good deal

---

18. Ibid., 29.

19. Complementarianism is the view that the Bible teaches that men and women are, while essentially equal in status and worth, given different roles in home and church.

20. Porter, *The New Puritans*, 31.

21. Ibid.

Are Sydney Anglicans Fundamentalists?

more accommodating than the practice of the Roman Catholic Church. Remarriage after divorce is not banned—it is, rather, that clergy are very reasonably required to be cautious and to seek episcopal approval in each instance. Since Scripture has some specific things to say on this issue, it seems unremarkable to find this policy in a Christian denomination. Sydney Anglicans talk about sex far less than outsiders sometimes think! However, it is true that an orthodox position on marriage—held by the majority of Anglican Christians today, contrary to Porter's claim—has been repeatedly upheld by the Sydney synod. Porter then repeats a piece of "anecdotal evidence" (her term) that is actually untrue: "it is now highly unlikely that a single man will be appointed rector of any Sydney parish, presumably for fear that his single state might mask an unacceptable sexual identity or that he might fall prey to sexual temptation."[22] There is no such policy. I cite Rev. John Gaunt, appointed rector of Blackheath in 2008, as a counterexample.[23]

"Separatism" is Porter's last check-box. She can only establish this by looking sideways at the evidence. She notes rightly that Sydney Anglicans are proudly countercultural, which she says "indicates a predisposition towards separatism."[24] However, it is scarcely a telling point. Christians have always seen themselves as countercultural in some way, since the earliest times. In any case, the label "separatism" invites the question "what separatism and on what grounds?" There have been many forms of separatism in Christian history justified for any number of reasons. The monastic movement is one such example. Porter quite overlooks the ongoing commitment of the Sydney diocese in any case to involvement in society—its commitment to justice and social welfare in which it continues to invest enormous resources. Sydney seeks the Christianization of society by inviting people to become Christians, not by spreading Christian values (so-called) abroad. That much is a given. But it is not tantamount to "separatism."

Porter's attempt to classify Sydney Anglicans as fundamentalists does not, then, succeed on its own terms.[25]

---

22. Ibid.

23. In addition, a number of single men have been appointed either as curate-in-charge or to congregational leadership in that time: Revs. Paul Dale, Evan McFarlane, Dave Rogers, Joe Wiltshire, and Steve Reimer.

24. Porter, *Sydney Anglicans*, 20.

25. After this chapter was initially written, Muriel Porter published a further book

On Not Being Fundamentalist

Like Donald Robinson, I do not think that Sydney Anglicans are fundamentalists. It may be that the critics of Sydney will call it "fundamentalist" in any case, of course, and see my protesting against it as typical of fundamentalist reactions to being called "fundamentalist." If the label "fundamentalist" means that they are sticking to the fundamentals of the Christian faith and submitting to the authority of the Scripture, then they ought to wear the label as a badge of honor. It is no more a term of disgrace than being called a rat was for the Rats of Tobruk. The term is being wielded in order to marginalize the Sydney position on a number of hot-button issues. After all, you don't have to take the ideas of fundamentalists seriously—you can't reason with them in any case. I hasten to add that I wouldn't want to be heard as not acknowledging that Sydney has played it pretty tough at times in the national Anglican Church. The reactions of Porter and others are not surprising, even if they are misguided; in one sense it is a description of Sydney's combative approach to intra-denominational politics more than anything else.

However, I do think there is such a thing as "fundamentalism," that it is a bad thing, and that Sydney Anglicans should resist the temptation to embrace it. There is after all that strange social phenomena that you can become what your critics say you are. It is possible to allow the critic's description to identify you. If the critic is someone whose views are completely at odds with those of the group, then it is possible to think that the critic's description of you is accurate, even though she thinks that the description is self-evidently bad. If she thinks it is bad, it must surely be good. What's more, the feeling of being isolated and attacked leads to a "circle the wagons" mentality. This defensiveness in a group is conducive to a fundamentalist mentality. It makes mature self-criticism nearly impossible.

I would accept that "fundamentalism" is descriptive of a kind of religious mentality that is in evidence most egregiously in a kind of epistemological double standard. That is, it is a mentality that confidently asserts the objectivity and interest-free status of its own reasoning while

---

about Sydney Anglicans: *Sydney Anglicans and the Threat to World Anglicanism: The Sydney Experiment*. This new work adds nothing new to the arguments of *The New Puritans*, especially on the issue of fundamentalism and has received some very tepid reviews. See, for example, Kaye, "Terms of Engagement"; Richardson, "Review: Muriel Porter."

at the same time decrying the prejudice and interest-laden nature of the reasoning of its opponents. This is the kind of "rationalism" that Harriet Harris decries in her book *Evangelicalism and Fundamentalism*.[26] Why is it bad? It is chiefly bad for spiritual rather than intellectual reasons. That is, it fails to be a posture of humble confidence rather than belligerence. It claims to know what it cannot. It is pastorally irresponsible, because it relies on intellectual shortcuts that people may accept for a time and then begin to doubt, to their spiritual detriment. I would also argue that it is bad because the fundamentalist mindset is actually *not* faithful to Scripture.

As I noted above, fundamentalism in the strict sense had its origins in a reaction to the modernism of the mainline churches and the academy in the 1920s. It exists because orthodox Protestant Christianity was being attacked at the very root. That is, the biblical criticism of the nineteenth century had led to a wholesale questioning of the normative Christian doctrines of the Trinity, the incarnation, the atonement and so on. The attacks of liberal Christianity on these fundamentals were themselves a type of rationalism—that is what the Anglo-Catholic writer John Henry Newman (1801–1890) called them in the 1840s. They were made in full confidence that the methods of academic theology could be sufficiently objective so as to establish verifiable truths—that we might be able to see through the supernaturalist accounts of the Gospels to the real Jesus, and so on. For someone like the German theologian Friedrich Schleiermacher (1768–1834), this rationalist approach had a rather more negative function in that it demolished the notion, held dearly in the seventeenth and eighteenth century, of orthodox Christianity as a faith established on rational grounds. The thought of David Hume (1711–1776) and then Immanuel Kant (1724–1805) had, as Schleiermacher saw it, proven that route to be a dead end.

But Schleiermacher did not despair. All this meant was that an account of Christian faith had to move into the more subjective and experiential realm. Christianity could not be primarily a set of truths to which one gives assent. Rather—and here Schleiermacher drew on his roots in German pietism, from which the evangelical John Wesley also drew—the Christian faith schooled the believer in the "feeling of absolute dependence." Schleiermacher gave a very sophisticated and highly original account of the Christian faith in these terms in his

26. Harris, *Fundamentalism and Evangelicals*, 133.

Glaubenslehre—perhaps the most remarkable piece of Christian theology of its era.[27] Christianity could self-describe as a spirituality, but it was not a coherent or plausible rational system.

So: the liberal Christianity of the Enlightenment reacts against the cerebral rationalism of the previous generation because it believes that the rationalist method has actually disproven orthodoxy. Instead, it starts to emphasize the experiential aspect of faith, which is all it has left to it. The evangelical movement of the same era, though conservative in belief, had also found real strength in its emphasis on the experiences of conviction of sin, conversion, and sanctification.

Conservative-minded Christians responded to this attack on the rational foundations of their beliefs by seeking a surer ground on which to stand. For John Henry Newman, a Calvinist evangelical from his youth, this meant seeking the embrace of tradition and the Church. In the US, the great Princeton theologians Charles Hodge (1797–1878) and B. B. Warfield (1851–1921), sought to defend orthodoxy on more rational grounds and through appeal to an inerrant Bible. Hodge and Warfield were men of the highest intellectual caliber. They had, however, accepted the terms of their opponents. Their defense of orthodoxy was on the same grounds that it had been attacked. That is to say: the claim was that rationalism had overcome orthodox Protestant Christianity and left us with no objective ground. Instead of challenging rationalism itself, Warfield and Hodge accepted the challenge to prove orthodoxy on a rational and apparently objective basis.

They were redoubtable. Warfield, who authored one of the original "Fundamentals," in particular remains an underrated scholar. His scholarly achievement—and personal integrity—was immense. But by the time of the 1920s, with modernity advanced even further in its attack on the rational basis for religious belief, those who became the fundamentalists had little room to move. They were right to insist on and appeal to the authority of Scripture. However they adopted a rather odd tactic. On the one hand, they attacked the presuppositions of their opponents, denying that there was such a thing as a purely rational approach. As they saw it, Darwin and Freud provided a convenient excuse to deny Christian teachings rather than having anything really objective to say. On the other hand, they insisted on the pure objectivity and rationality of their own views, based on Scripture. A rationalism based

27. Schleiermacher, *The Christian Faith*.

on Scripture was acceptable, where a rationalism based on nature was ruled illegitimate.

What is overlooked in this picture is the fact that "rationality," as such, does not exist without people who think. Scripture read with the eyes of faith provides, as John Calvin says, the "spectacles" through which all reality may be rightly observed. But this was not merely a rational thought process in his description of it. It was an operation of the Holy Spirit on corrupted human reason.

We can see from this account that the emergence of the fundamentalist mentality was more a matter of *epistemology*—what and how we can know things—than it was about specific theological convictions. Appeal to the supreme authority of Scripture does not make one a fundamentalist. What might rightly be called "fundamentalism" appeals to the authority of Scripture and establishes that authority by appeal to a kind of rational argument that is supposedly not exposed to the effects of sin on human knowing in the way that all other reasoning is. The privilege of making such an argument is not granted to its opponents, who are held to be in the sway of some agenda or other.

Under blistering attack from other parts of the Anglican world, the retreat to a fundamentalist mentality might become a real temptation for Sydney Anglicans. But it will not do. If they were to adopt a fundamentalist mentality, it would be to their own detriment. In a 2002 speech, Peter Jensen commented:

> I am not a fundamentalist, but I have a sympathy towards fundamentalism. I believe that we should all share that sympathy so that we can gain an insight into what creates the phenomenon. My point is this: modernity is worse than fundamentalism. I would argue that the exaltation of human reason has led to a society in the grip of ceaseless and yet apparently purposeless change; we are being churned in the untamable waters of history; we are (to vary the metaphor), suffering from spiritual vertigo. From the Christian point of view, modernity involves the misery of relativistic and shallow values, based on a profound misunderstanding of who we are.[28]

---

28. Jensen, "Fundamentalism."

Certainly, if mere concession to the agendas of modernity is the alternative, then fundamentalism has its attractions. Yet as modernism's twin, fundamentalism exalts human reason in its own way, too.

If appeal to the authority of Scripture does not make one a fundamentalist, then neither does confidence in one's own theological positions. Christians of all stripes are called on to affirm the creeds week by week. There is a kind of insistent doubting skepticism that is its own terrible vice, as James the brother of Jesus says (Jas 1). However, it is a grave *theological* mistake to accord one's theological convictions the finality that only the judgment of God can give them. Belligerence is not the necessary complement of confident conviction.

Let me be clear. One does not eschew the sobriquet "fundamentalist" on account of wishing to look respectable. The term is treated with such a mixture of alarm and contempt in the contemporary world that you could be forgiven for not wanting to be the target of such opprobrium. But "respectability" is not a category that ought to interest Christians if it means compromise of the gospel of Jesus Christ. Christians are those for whom being killed by one's neighbors for what one believes is a consideration. After all, it was not dignity or status that Christ himself pursued. Respectability is not a Christian category. If being fundamentalist means "not one of the respectable people," then I would happily accept it as a label.

But the great mistake would be to read any criticism as vindication, and lack of respectability as a goal to be pursued for its own sake. Criticism may be unfair persecution and a sign that you are on the right track. It may also be fair. It is extraordinarily difficult for the group under strong criticism to think clearly about itself—the criticism has the effect of making clear self-analysis difficult. An internal and loyal critic may be seen to be siding with the outsider. The critic from outside tries to isolate the object of her derision from the great stream of Christian tradition. To accept their description is to find oneself in the lonely position that E. J. Carnell spoke about in the 1950s.

Strangely (perhaps), the remedy for a potential fundamentalism is not anything other than reading Scripture again and again. Sydney Anglicans must continue to work on Scripture and being faithful to it if they are not to become fundamentalist, in fact. What do I mean? I mean that the theological conviction that God is at work in Scripture by his Spirit to bring about the renewal and repentance of his people is exactly right. The persistent and faithful reader of the Bible must be renewed in his or her mindset (Rom 12:1–2). The reader of Scripture is at once more deeply convicted about the reality and presence of God in Christ for the salvation of many, and of their own fragility. As it turns out, an approach to reading the Bible that allows for this kind of effect has been used by Sydney Anglicans for many years. What that approach is, and where it comes from, is the subject of the next chapter.

three

What the Bible Means: The Significance of "Biblical Theology"

What the Bible Means

How do you get from "what the Bible *meant*" to "what the Bible *means*"? The conviction of Protestants since the Swiss Reformer John Calvin (1509–1564) is that the way to interpret and apply Scripture must emerge from Scripture itself. The development of what became known as "Biblical Theology" at Moore College was tailored to meet the need for an approach to the Bible that would enable each text of the Bible to speak in its own way without a theological or ideological grid being imposed on it. The work of Donald Robinson and his students Bill Dumbrell and Graeme Goldsworthy has been crucial for shaping how Sydney Anglicans think about and preach from the Bible.

The apostle Paul wrote that "All Scripture is God-breathed and is useful for teaching, rebuking, correcting and training in righteousness" (2 Tim 3:16). Since the very early days of the church, Christian people have been determined to see the whole Bible as the divine and authoritative word. Christians sit under the *whole* of Scripture. But the Bible has some very strange passages in it. Any Christian will readily admit that parts of the Old Testament are quite baffling, at least on first reading. If all Scripture is useful, what is one to do with the command not to eat pelicans (Lev 11:18)? Or, even when an Old Testament narrative is quite straightforwardly written, it remains to be seen how the story is going to shape Christian living. The solution for the Alexandrian linguist, philosopher, and theologian Origen (185–254) was to introduce an *allegorical* method of reading the text, which meant that, in principle, you could apply to any Old Testament text. The allegorical reading of Scripture was championed by theologians as worthy at Augustine of Hippo (354–430).

This allegorical or spiritualizing way of reading Scripture arises out of a desire to apply the whole Bible to the Christian, but it leads to some curious results. Graeme Goldsworthy opens his book *Gospel and Kingdom* with the fictional story of "Ken," who had heard a speaker at a children's rally present the story of David and Goliath.[1] The dramatized presentation was accurate, and even delightful, but the application of the story was deeply disturbing for poor Ken. The actor playing Goliath had peeled off successive strips of cardboard to reveal different sins—the "Goliaths" we all have to face. The actor playing David, for his part, wielded a sling called "faith" loaded with five stones called "obedience," "service," "Bible reading," "prayer" and "fellowship." Of course, the text of the Bible itself gives absolutely no indication that this sort of symbolism is intended by the author. Indeed, the cute allegory breaks down because only one of the stones is needed to kill the giant—and we aren't told which one!

In this little story, Goldsworthy encapsulates the millennia-old problem of biblical interpretation. What makes ancient Scripture God's word for the church and for the Christian here today? How does what it meant relate to what it means? For Sydney Anglicans, the development of the "Biblical Theology" approach has been the answer. And the story of Biblical Theology in Sydney begins with the career of Donald Robinson, lecturer in New Testament and vice principal at Moore College, and subsequently archbishop of Sydney from 1982–1991.

Donald Robinson and Biblical Theology

Robinson was educated not at Moore but at Sydney University, where he studied Greek, and then at Cambridge, where he completed his theological training. He was exposed there to the finest English-speaking biblical scholarship of the day including C. H. Dodd (1884–1973) and C. F. D. Moule (1908–2007). His commitment to evangelicalism, honed

---

1. Goldsworthy, *The Goldsworthy Trilogy*, 7.

by many years of involvement in the high school movement Crusaders and the Sydney University Evangelical Union (SUEU), remained firm in his participation in the Cambridge Inter-Collegiate Christian Union (CICCU) and on his return to Australia he taught at Moore until he became bishop of Parramatta in 1972.

Robinson was an expert linguist and an exegetical master with a remorseless determination to read the text without the white noise of traditional expectation. He felt that his evangelical commitment to the supreme authority of the Bible actually licensed this exegetical freedom. Along with Broughton Knox (1916–1994), principal of Moore College from 1959–1985, he was the evangelical bulwark against the powerful Anglo-Catholicism that sought to dominate the Australian Church in the 1950s, 60s, and 70s. Robinson's 1981 book *Faith's Framework*, a version of his Moore College lectures for 1979, were the distillation of his approach to Scripture as a whole.[2]

Robinson himself saw that the influence of Dodd, the Swiss biblical scholar Oscar Cullman, and an Anglo-Catholic priest named Gabriel Hebert (1886–1963) as shaping the introduction of Biblical Theology. Assigned by principal Marcus Loane to teach a first year course known as "Special Doctrine," Robinson transformed it into an introduction and overview of the Bible as a way of orienting the students to the discipline of theology and "to stimulate students'" general reading of the Bible."[3] In the midst of developing this course, his interaction with Father Hebert (who lived in South Australia during the 1950s) was crucial. Hebert was a stern critic of evangelical biblical scholarship, especially as it had been represented by IVP's *New Bible Commentary*—to which Robinson himself had contributed the chapter on Jonah. In his book *Fundamentalism and the Church of God* he argued that the *New Bible Commentary* was "weak and timid in exegesis, lacked a full world view, an integrated Biblical theology and an adequate view of the church."[4] For Robinson, an encounter with Hebert at a conference at St. Paul's College, Sydney University in 1952 was a seminal moment for the development of the Biblical Theology course, and indeed the whole notion of "Biblical Theology" at Moore. As Robinson put it: ". . . our Biblical Theology course

---

2. Robinson, *Faith's Framework*.
3. Robinson, "Origins and Unresolved Tensions," 7.
4. Ibid., 6.

was being fashioned in the midst of an on-going debate with Dr Hebert himself . . . on these very questions."⁵

What is perhaps surprising about the development of the Biblical Theology course is the way in which it was shaped by interaction with non-evangelicals. It was bred of Robinson's genuinely intellectual approach. He was a man of firm evangelical convictions, but he listened to and even learned from some of evangelicalism's strongest critics. Biblical Theology was the result of Robinson's intellectual eclecticism as well as of his commitment to the authority of Scripture. He was certainly sensitive to Hebert's accusation that evangelicals made too great a use of proof texts. As he wrote, with a slight bristle in his tone: "I do not think that there was ever any danger of our brand of conservative evangelicalism espousing a use of Scripture which took statements or verses out of their biblical contexts."⁶

The Biblical Theology course as it developed divided the biblical story in three stages. The first was from the promise to Abraham in Genesis 12 to the realization of the promise in the kingdom of Solomon. Following the decline of Solomon's kingdom, the second stage it discerned stretched forward to the end of the period of the prophets. The third stage equated roughly to the New Testament itself—from the coming of Christ to the consummation of the age. It was perhaps unusual to make Solomon's reign such a fulcrum, but Robinson had noted in his studies the prominence of the covenant promises to David in 2 Samuel 7 which concerned his son and what he might achieve. The glory of Solomon's reign in 1 King 3–10 is certainly a high point of peace, prosperity and power in Israel's history—a high point to which there is ascendance and from which there is general decline.

The idea of "promise and fulfillment" was naturally a concept that drove a Biblical Theology of the kind Robinson was urging, because it showed how the two testaments were related. Robinson admitted that the treatment of the New Testament in his course was rather restricted because of the emphasis on showing how certain passages of the New Testament made reference to the Old.⁷ One of the remarkable emphases to emerge from this treatment of the New Testament was the way in which fulfillment of the Old Testament expectations was "now and not

---

5. Ibid.
6. Ibid.
7. Ibid., 11.

yet." The New Testament speaks about the fulfillment of the promises but also about the coming further fulfillment of them. As Robinson himself noted, there were a number of contemporary theological treatments of Christian hope emerging in the 1950s and 60s (such as those of Jürgen Moltmann and Wolfhart Pannenberg), and a new awareness of the eschatological nature of the New Testament vision for Christian life.

The approach pioneered by Robinson became known as "Biblical Theology." The title is not entirely satisfactory, for it is also the title of the "Biblical Theology Movement" in biblical studies which was prominent in the 1940s through to the 1960s. Like Gabriel Hebert, these scholars such Gerhard von Rad (1901–1971) and G. Ernest Wright (1909–1974) were conscious of liberal and critical presuppositions and methods in biblical interpretation, but were at the same time concerned to read the Bible as a theological document—something they felt had been neglected by the older liberalism. It grew as a parallel to the work of neo-orthodox systematic theologians such as Karl Barth (1886–1968) and Emil Brunner (1889–1966) in Europe and Richard (1894–1962) and Reinhold Niebuhr (1892–1971) in the US. The Biblical Theologians of midcentury sought to understand the Bible as a fully human book that demanded investigation by the proper tools of historical criticism and yet could still be seem as the unique witness to the divine Word.

Study of the Bible by a previous generation of liberal scholars had concentrated on attempting to discern the (often multiple and complex) sources behind the development of the biblical text. For example, Julius Wellhausen (1844–1918) identified four intertwined sources in the book of Genesis and labeled them "J," "E," "P" and "D" according to what he felt were their different agendas and literary styles. Having reconstructed these sources, they were then interpreted from the standpoint of the historical or cultural context of their creation. It was this method that was entirely in the ascendency in academic scholarship on the Bible by the time of the 1920s in both Europe and America. However, it was hard to see what good such methods of biblical interpretation were supposed to do for churches and for the people in them. The Biblical Theology Movement was not willfully deaf to the so-called gains in historical-critical scholarship, as the fundamentalists were, but it was seeking to recover something viable from the debris that it had left behind. It wanted to move beyond liberalism while retaining its methods.

To do this it could not return to the older Protestant orthodox notion of inspiration. Instead it found help in the neo-orthodox description of Scripture as a witness to the revelation of God in Christ. By this doctrine, Biblical Theology claimed that it could have its biblical cake and eat it too. It was able to maintain a vigorous polemic against the sterility of liberalism while at the same time evading fundamentalism. Against liberalism it claimed that instead of making the Christian faith into a set of universal and timeless principles, it was able to listen to the powerfully particular voice of the Bible. Instead of using categories drawn from Greek thought, the Biblical Theologians sought to understand the Bible and its theological framework from within. It emphasized as it did so the importance of discerning Hebraic, and not Greek, thought patterns. These strikingly unique patterns of thought emerge especially from comparative studies of the Old Testament with the religion of Israel's neighbors in the Ancient Near East.

Unlike the older liberalism, the Biblical Theology Movement held that Scripture was a unity. In reaction to the atomization of the Bible, it attempted to deal with both Testaments together. This was done, however, through an appeal to history rather than to the unity of the divine voice in Scripture or any similar notion. The concept of "revelation in history" was at once a repudiation of a conservative insistence that the words of Scripture themselves were revelatory and the liberal notion that the Bible marks a record of evolving religious discovery. God's self-disclosure was in the events, and not in any emerging propositional content referring to such events.

By the mid-1960s, however, the Biblical Theology Movement had started to wane. Biblical scholars Brevard Childs (1923–2007) and James Barr both noted this fading away. Leaning so heavily on historical-critical methods and yet wanting to hold a roughly orthodox theological position, it seems that Biblical Theology of this type was inherently unstable. As Brevard Childs wrote: "the historical-critical method is an inadequate method of studying the Bible as the Scriptures of the church."[8] The emphasis on reconstruction of the historical background of the emergence of the biblical text made it very hard for the Biblical Theologians to achieve their own aim of discovering what the

---

8. Childs, *Biblical Theology in Crisis*, 141.

text means for today. Furthermore, the notion of "revelation in history" was exposed as ambiguous at best by a number of scholars including Langdon Gilkey (1919–2004) and James Barr.

While he accepted much of the criticism that had been leveled against the Biblical Theology Movement, the Yale Old Testament scholar Childs[9] made a resolute effort to retrieve some of its finer fruit. He accordingly developed a "canonical" approach to reading Scripture, by which he interacted with premodern as well as modern exegetes. Treatment of the text in its final form is the aim of the canonical-critical method, although it uses historical-critical scholarship of the text's creation where it is relevant. Childs bravely attempted to do genuinely *biblical* scholarship rather than merely Old Testament scholarship, bridging the Testaments when it was unfashionable to do so in the academy. It was somewhat of a lone hand. The prevailing fashion for much of the 60s, 70s, and 80s was to highlight the supposed cacophony of the voices that are heard in Scripture. In the work of British New Testament scholar James Dunn (1939–), for example, the sheer disunity of the Bible became almost the very point of it—it was communicating a message of the inclusion of widely disparate points of view.

Thus Moore College's own "Biblical Theology" emerged at the same time as the "Biblical Theology Movement" was under severe attack. Yet because Moore's version of Biblical Theology was not dependent on the historical-critical method—even though Donald Robinson was certainly abreast of its claims—it was able to continue to develop as a viable discipline while the Biblical Theology Movement was in disarray. Likewise, there were North American scholars from the Reformed tradition following the lead of Geerhardus Vos (1862–1949) who were continuing to work out a notion of "Biblical Theology" apart from dependence on liberal biblical scholarship and without a concomitant denial of the inspiration of Scripture.

Graeme Goldsworthy and Gospel and Kingdom

Robinson left Moore for the episcopacy in 1972, leaving his task to a young Graeme Goldsworthy. Studious and quick-witted, the trumpet-playing Goldsworthy was an Old Testament scholar with a doctorate

---

9. Childs was a personal friend of Donald Robinson.

from Union Seminary in Virginia. When he in turn left Moore for pastoral ministry in Queensland, he produced a little book that is still the standard work on Biblical Theology: *Gospel and Kingdom* (1981).[10] The brilliance of this very short book is not in its complexity nor in the sweetness of the prose. Goldsworthy wrote it for use in a pastoral context at the Anglican church of St Stephen's Coorparoo, Brisbane. It is a book that was given to me as a teenager on a camp in 1986 and which took an afternoon to grasp. I have taught its contents to thirteen year olds. But I remember the feeling that what this book was saying was so obvious that it was amazing that I hadn't seen it before. Its genius is that it moves people from a Sunday school understanding of Scripture to a mature adult understanding of Scripture by putting it all in a coherent and plausible whole

What Robinson and Goldsworthy taught was not a novelty in fact. The great French-Swiss Reformer John Calvin had described an approach to reading Scripture that took it is a unified whole, with Jesus Christ as it "scope"—who in turn learned from the church father Irenaeus (d. 202) and indeed from the way the apostles themselves made use of the Old Testament. The Old Testament must be read by Christians as pointing to Jesus in whom "all God's promises are 'yes.'" The Bible is not a collection of disconnected proof texts, but is unified by the history that it narrates—the history of Israel, in the first instance, which remarkably becomes the history of the whole of humankind. The great "covenant" passages of the Old Testament—Genesis 12 and 15 (Abraham), Exodus 19–20 (Moses), 2 Samuel 7 (David) and Jeremiah 31 (Jeremiah)—are the lodestars for the reader and help to form a coherent picture of the whole text by which almost any individual passage or book can be interpreted. The Bible unfolds its story as a "progressive revelation" such that what God reveals about himself is fuller and more complete the further along in the Biblical narrative we read. Both the unfolding nature of the Bible's disclosure of God's character and purposes and the climactic function of Jesus Christ as a fulfillment of all the promises of God are expressed in the three short verses that open the letter to the Hebrews:

> In the past God spoke to our forefathers through the prophets at many times and in various ways, but in these last days

---

10. *Gospel and Kingdom* is now published in Goldsworthy, *The Goldsworthy Trilogy*.

> he has spoken to us by his Son, whom he appointed heir of all things, and through whom he made the universe. The Son is the radiance of God's glory and the exact representation of his being, sustaining all things by his powerful word. After he had provided purification for sins, he sat down at the right hand of the Majesty in heaven.

"Biblical Theology" remains a standard first year course at Moore College. It is unusual in theological education to have a subject whose task is to integrate the two components of Scripture. New Testament and Old Testament are, in most theological colleges, taught as separate disciplines—as they are at Moore. But Moore College's students learn to read the New in the light of the Old and the Old in the light of the New—as many of the great expositors of Christian history have done. Furthermore, Moore's correspondence course, the Preliminary Theological Certificate, starts with a subject called "Introduction to the Bible" in which this integrated way of reading the Bible is explained. This course has been studied by thousands of students all over the world, and has been translated into Chinese, Spanish, and Arabic. It has, in a sense, become a flagship subject.

At its best, Biblical Theology is a pedagogical marvel. It gives the student a way of integrating his or her theological studies around Scripture—and it does so persuasively. Biblical Theology sets up a model that is strong enough to provide coherence and yet loose enough to open up the interpretation of Scripture rather than to shut it down. It allows us to read each part of Scripture on its own terms (in the first instance)—the Psalms as Psalms, the law as law, and so on. But it is also shows us how the rich variety of these parts work together to form a greater whole. It is a big vision: Biblical Theology shows the breadth and profundity of God's work in salvation history.

And so, Biblical Theology is actually a form of what is usually called "hermeneutics." That is, it is an approach to the interpretation of the texts of Scripture. But this approach claims to be the approach the text itself generates. It is an outworking of the Protestant principle that Scripture ought to interpret Scripture. It stands obstinately against the "special interest" hermeneutics that dominated academia (especially in the US) at the end of the twentieth century. The Biblical Theology approach does not completely disallow that different perspectives—feminist, post-colonial, liberationist, and so on—might have something fresh to say about the text, or that these approaches may in fact shed new light on the text. Theologians who advocate Biblical Theology must of course be alert to the charge that they are merely sanctifying their own perspective. But if the text itself disappears beneath the overlay of interpretative points-of-view—as it often seems to—then, unsurprisingly, Biblical Theology advocates lose interest. The moment hermeneutics becomes about something other than the text it is interpreting, then we might as well shut the Bible and discuss our competing ideologies. Being aware of one's own subjectivity in the reading process is necessary for true reading. The theologian is helped massively by the long history of reading the text in question to which she might easily refer. But recognizing the subjective aspect of reading does not mean that reading becomes a matter of mere subjectivity. Postmodern hermeneutics have had a contribution to make, but they have not erased the text altogether.

For many years, Biblical Theology of the type introduced by Robinson and promoted by Goldsworthy sounded like an Australian quirk borne of isolation from the rest of the world. Since the mid-1980s, however, the Biblical Theology approach has been surprisingly vindicated by the way in which scholars from a whole variety of backgrounds have adopted similar methods. The work of Tom (N. T.) Wright (1948–), sometime bishop of Durham, burst on to the scholarly scene in the early 1990s with the publication of his *Climax of the Covenant*.[11] Wright's background was within the solidly evangelical Oxford Inter-Collegiate Christian Union. His early theological writings showed a determinedly Reformed bent in terms of the solidly Calvinistic doctrines he followed. It was the Reformed determination to read the whole of Scripture as God's word that left the indelible mark on Wright's writing—just as it had in Sydney. He showed again and again how the Old Testament and historical background were essential for an understanding of the New Testament. The strong critique of some aspects of Wright's work offered by some Sydney Anglican scholars masks the great similarities between the approaches they share as a matter of fact.

More broadly, since the mid-1990s there has been a growing group of scholars including Kevin Vanhoozer, Daniel Treier, Francis Watson, Gregory Jones, and others, who have outlined what they have called "the theological interpretation of Scripture." This movement is a grandchild of the Swiss theologian Karl Barth and heavily influenced

---

11. Wright, *The Climax of the Covenant*.

by Brevard Childs and his "canonical criticism." Amongst these scholars, the excitement of discovery—or I should say *re*discovery—is palpable. The aim of this new approach is to reposition study of the Bible as "the joint responsibility of all the theological disciplines and of the whole people of God."[12] For too long, a turf war has been conducted in academic theology as to whose job it is to handle the text of Scripture that has only resulted in the loss of the sense that the text might have anything to say about its chief subject, namely, *God*. Theological interpreters seek to know about God from Scripture. And while cutting no scholarly corners, they seek to hear what God is saying in Scripture to the church.

The notion of "theological interpretation of Scripture" remains a broad and unsystematic one and includes within it scholars from all denominational backgrounds and numerous theological perspectives. It would be accurate to say that the various scholars involved share concerns and express them in different methods. Yet these concerns are similar to the concerns that led to the creation of the Biblical Theology course at Moore a generation or more ago. The appearance of the "theological interpretation" movement (if it may be so called) is a vindication of Robinson and Goldsworthy. But it is also an invitation to go further.

Where To Now?

The Biblical Theology approach remains one of Moore's great strengths. Providentially, at the beginning of the twenty-first century, the hermeneutical approach pioneered by Robinson in dialogue with Hebert in the 1950s is not a theological tributary but is very much part of the international mainstream. The potential of this approach is only just being realized. Yet at Moore, Biblical Theology is still a first-year introductory course designed to be a lens through which other parts of the theological curriculum are viewed. In practice, it is then integrated throughout the curriculum. But if Biblical Theology as a subject in its own right remains at this introductory level and is not given the opportunity to be exposed to the remarkable and extensive work being done in the field, then it risks becoming a very limited glimpse rather than a panoramic vista. If students are not exposed to the wide range of

---

12. Vanhoozer, Treier, and Wright, *Theological Interpretation of the New Testament*, 21.

writings now on offer, Biblical Theology will not be refined but remain thick-grained and coarse. If students are not encouraged to pursue the study of Biblical Theology at a senior and even at a research level, then it will not progress as a discipline in line with the other disciplines.[13]

"Biblical Theology" could be a mediating discipline between systematic theology on the one hand and biblical studies on the other, making a fuller, more *theological* reading of Scripture possible.[14] It should not become the pretext for an eclipse of the separate discipline of systematic theology altogether. This temptation lies somewhat in the title "Biblical Theology" itself, which, read with a rather triumphalist tone, could be heard as claiming the redundancy of other types of theology. What theology is there if it isn't "biblical" theology? As it stands, Biblical Theology is frequently taught by biblical studies experts and not in concert with systematic theologians. The potential weakness here is that the specifically *theological* foundations and commitments upon which a Biblical theological method is built go unexpressed and unchecked. Furthermore, the systematic theologian is always alert to the way in which the creeds and definitions of church history and the work of later theologians can help us in understanding the text.

One other potential distraction is to see the various descriptions of the Bible's literary unity as establishing its theological coherence, rather than the other way around. The Bible's unity is ultimately a *theological* understanding. It coheres not because it corresponds to a certain interpretational scheme but because it is the work of a single, divine author. This singularity finds its outworking in the centrality of Jesus Christ to the Christian understanding of Scripture. Whatever one might say about the framework and literary structure of Scripture, it cannot be Holy Scripture if it is not Christocentric. However, this might mean that a number of themes or schemes can be described in it. One theme may not exhaust all that Scripture says about Christ. Likewise, any scheme needs to be aware that it highlights some passages and diminishes some others. Goldsworthy wrote persuasively about the wisdom literature and its relationship to Biblical Theology in his book *Gospel*

---

13. Happily, there are now offerings in Biblical Theology at fourth year and MA level.

14. "Systematic" Theology names the discipline that deals with the knowledge of God at a conceptual, integrative, and summative way.

and Wisdom[15] as a response to just this kind of accusation against him. Confusion over whether Biblical Theology commits you to a presupposition about Scripture or to a particular reading of the coherence of Scripture is a potentially limiting factor.

A commitment to Biblical Theology has been (humanly speaking) the secret to the theological robustness of the Moore College education. It keeps the whole theological enterprise rooted in the revelation of God himself and focused on its purpose to serve his church. Sydney Anglican preachers have the means at their disposal to preach from any part of Scripture. That is why a call to a renewed focus on the unity and coherence of Scripture and on the marvelous way in which it reveals Christ to us with such profundity is never superfluous.

A commitment to Biblical Theology is only worthwhile inasmuch as it is based on an understanding that the God's revelation is for us today. Just what that understanding entails is the concern of the next chapter.

---

15. Goldsworthy, *Gospel and Wisdom*.

four

Propositional Revelation the Only Revelation? Scripture and Revelation in the Diocese of Sydney

The Only Revelation?

In 1960, the then principal of Moore College, Dr. Broughton Knox, penned a small article for the Australian journal *The Reformed Theological Review* entitled "Propositional Revelation, the Only Revelation."[1] It was Knox at his provocative, polemical best. Less than four thousand words long, it was the sort of article that becomes a landmark—not the least because of its adamant slogan of a title. And so it became. Here was, it seemed, another *sola* to add to the Reformation *solas*—a manifesto for evangelicals against the sweeping tide of liberal theology. Scripture alone. Faith alone. Grace alone. Propositional revelation alone?

This short piece elicited an almost immediate response from the Melbourne theologian Eric Osborn in the *Australian Biblical Review*.[2] Osborn argued that by asserting *propositional* revelation, Knox was presenting a greatly reduced version of the nature of divine communication. Osborn further compared Knox's argument with that of John Anderson (1893–1962) the well-known atheist professor of philosophy

---

1. In *Broughton Knox Selected Works*, vol 1.
2. Osborn, "Realism and Revelation," 29–37.

at Sydney University, whose philosophical outlook could be described by the epithet "logical positivism."[3]

Osborn misunderstood Knox, but Knox did not make it easy. As we shall see, Knox's use of the term "propositional" was perhaps ill-advised; both his enemies and his friends have taken him to mean something quite specific when he meant something rather broad. Knox was not a "logical positivist," though he was influenced by some features of logical positivism: his wide definition of "propositional," which simply means "linguistic" or "verbal," is not as narrow as that of the logical positivists. What's more, the use of the word "only" was hyperbole. As a result of the confusion, however, this small article has had a distorting rather than clarifying influence on how Sydney Anglican theology has sometimes perceived itself, and how it has been perceived.

Following Knox, Sydney Anglican writers and teachers insist that the Bible is God's word: that in its words, God *speaks* to human beings so that they may hear and understand. Though he himself is beyond human comprehension, God's self-revelation is intelligible. What can this mean? And is it defensible in the light of alternatives put forward by others?

Peter Carnley and Mystery

One such alternative is found in the 2004 book by former archbishop of Perth and primate of the Anglican Church in Australia, Peter Carnley, *Reflections in Glass*,[4] a work in which he specifically targets the "Sydney" sort of Anglicanism on a number of fronts. The opening chapter of the book, "God: Manifestation or Mystery?" most helpfully and elegantly outlines Carnley's theology of revelation and the ground for the critique of evangelicalism on the various controversial issues that follows. Carnley sets up a contrast between the view that God is made known in an intelligible way ("manifestation") and the view that he remains a mystery. He begins with the stereotype of Anglicans as lacking any firm convictions, one that has given rise to much humor over the years (he cites the UK sitcom *The Vicar of Dibley*) but that, according to Carnley, contains more than a grain of truth. Anglicans are, he says, character-

---

3. For a lively account of Anderson's career and influence, see Franklin, *Corrupting the Youth*.

4. Carnley, *Reflections in Glass*.

istically reticent to make theological truth claims. Outside the creeds, all sorts of personal beliefs may be admitted, but Anglicans refrain with humility from saying more than this about God. Speak of him we must—but with the greatest of care. This is why, as he explains, he does not like the term "liberal": because it implies a positive dependence on human reason, which Carnley sees as limited and flawed.

This reticence is grounded on a primary, and utterly orthodox, theological truth: the sheer transcendence of God. This is the "index of Christian orthodoxy."[5] God is not to be reduced to our statements about him nor contained by our thoughts. He is "an infinite mystery, an ineffable, transcendent reality."[6] This dogma is "essential to the understanding of the ethos of Anglicanism";[7] and it is particularly so for the "progressive" "orthodoxy" being road-tested here. This single truth, says Carnley, has massive implications for our speech about God. When human beings talk of God they necessarily use metaphor—rock, wind, fire, shepherd, father. "We project these images onto a heavenly screen," he says.[8]

In a slightly confusing way, he then introduces the tradition of "apophatic" theology. For Carnley, such negative theology—speaking of God by saying what he is not—is really the only possible result of proper engagement with the transcendent mystery of God. With the Eastern Orthodox churches (frequently given praiseworthy mention by Carnley), he claims that Anglicans share this essential tradition. God is essentially "a hidden God"[9]—unknowable and incomprehensible, more to be apprehended than comprehended: "At the end of the day, we must confess that 'God as God is in God's self' is an unsearchable mystery."[10] Even the Incarnation of the Word of God, in his view, does not enlighten us: we are given in the person and work of Jesus more mystery.[11]

In addition, human reason itself must be seen as limited, halting, and incomplete. We should be reminded by this of our intellectual poverty as human beings. The implication that flows is that our theological

5. Ibid., 31.
6. Ibid., 25.
7. Ibid., 27.
8. Ibid., 28.
9. Ibid., 29.
10. Ibid.
11. Ibid., 30.

language—in fact, all human language—is always to be limited. Worship of God should precede speaking of God. In the end, our knowledge of God can only ever be blurred and fragmentary. Although Carnley allows that there ought to be positive doctrinal statements about God, such as are contained in the great creeds of the church, it is not at all clear from his reasoning how these statements might be possible. He admits it rather than affirms it.

Part of the problem here is that Carnley imagines that evangelicals do not agree with him when in fact they do. Much of this chapter is not really in dispute: the sheer transcendence of God is a thoroughly biblical and orthodox teaching, as Carnley demonstrates (cf. Rom 11:33). I would concur—of course!—that our theological discourse must take second place to our prayerful devotion to God, and amidst an attitude of the utmost humility. Evangelical Anglican stalwart J. I. Packer would agree that we *apprehend* more than comprehend God; that our feeble human knowledge could never contain him.[12] Carnley's description of the nature of God is thoughtful and stimulating.

I would challenge, however, Carnley's theological reasoning from this basic truth. The dichotomy he posits—"manifestation" or "mystery"—is a false one. Scripture speaks of an invisible God (John 1:18) and a hidden God (Isa 45:15), but does not present an unknowable God. In fact, "No one has ever seen God. It is God the only Son, who is close to the Father's heart, who has made him known" (John 1:18).

The incarnation of the word of God gives God himself to us. God makes himself known to us—not in a way that is exhaustive, but in a way that is true and intelligible. The Nicene theologians—who could be more orthodox than they?—would not have agreed with this Carnleyan skepticism, primarily because the revelation of God in Christ as Father gives us a real knowledge of God as God is in himself. Here is what renowned Scottish theologian T. F. Torrance (1913–2007) writes:

> [Athanasius and Hilary] . . . differentiated themselves here sharply from the thesis of Basileides, the Gnostic of Alexandria,

---

12. In his classic article from 1973 "What did the Cross Achieve? The Logic of Penal Substitutionary Atonement," Packer wrote: "Christian speech verbalizes the apprehended mystery of God by using a distinctive non-representational 'picture-language.' This consists of parables, analogies, metaphors and images piled up in balance with each other, as in the Bible itself (from which this language is first learned), and all pointing to the reality of God's presence and action in order to evoke awareness of it and response to it" (10–11).

who taught, with reference to Plato's statement that God is beyond all being, that we cannot say anything about what God is, but can only say something about what he is not. It was pointed out by Gregory Nazianzen, however, that if we cannot say anything positive about what God is, we really cannot say anything accurate about what he is not.[13]

The Nicene theologians added that the incarnation gives us a point of access to God that is both "in God himself and in our creaturely existence."[14] In Christ, God gives us true knowledge of himself. Basil of Caesarea (who Carnley cites approvingly) recognized that though God is ineffable, this does not mean he is unintelligible: "We confess that we know what is knowable of God and yet that what we know reaches beyond our comprehension."[15]

We see here that despite the fact that we cannot contain God by our reason, we most certainly do have knowledge of him. Basil explained that this was by means of the Holy Spirit, the "Spirit of knowledge," who bestowed on true worshipers true knowledge of God.[16] In the language of Ephesians 2:18, "through Jesus Christ we are given access to the Father in one Spirit."

That is not to say that this knowledge of God is total or totally comprehensible. However, it is to allow a great deal more than Carnley will. Even though Athanasius and Hilary would be as cautious as he in making statements about God, they felt it necessary to speak in keeping with what they saw as the truth. They

> were reflecting what had been done at the Council of Nicaea when the fathers sought to give accurate and exact expression to the heart and substance of the evangelical message as conveyed through the Holy Scriptures, and thus brought to light the underlying pattern of the truth of the Gospel in *the light of which the Scriptures themselves become more intelligible to us.*[17]

It was the heretical Arians who taught that God was still utterly unknown, even after Christ. What we read in the New Testament is a confidence that believers, with the aid of the Spirit, will know God, and

13. Torrance, *The Trinitarian Faith*, 50.
14. Ibid., 52.
15. *Epistles* 235.2, cited in Torrance, *The Trinitarian Faith*, 214.
16. *On the Holy Spirit* 27, in Torrance, *The Trinitarian Faith*, 214.
17. Torrance, *The Trinitarian Faith*, 58.

know cognitively about God—that there has been a remarkable, but in its way comprehensible, revelation of God in the Word and in the words of the gospel. This is what the Nicene theologians so strongly asserted against the Gnostic and Arian heretics.

Human speech about God must recognize its limitations, naturally. God is not "a rock"; he does not have arms or a face. But are all the words in Scripture in the same category? Does Christ's speech fit into the category of human speech about God? When he calls his father "Father," is this merely a human groping after the divine? I assume that Carnley would say "yes," based on what he has written. The Nicene fathers and orthodox theologians before them and after them saw in the Scriptures a *given* language about God that enables us with appropriate hesitancy and reserve to speak positively about and to the Almighty. Otherwise, we pray to the void.

However, if we follow Carnley, the revelation we have of God is no revelation at all. God is not with us, does not give himself to us, but comes so cloaked that we must doubt whether we have seen his glory at all. What is disturbing here is that in the name of humility he presumes to look behind the revelation of God in Christ and Scripture and say that God is actually not as he is revealed to us. Revelation is really deception! In revelation God gives us nothing of his true self but only a masquerade. While Carnley does claim that he holds to positive statements about God, it is unclear to me, especially given his hermeneutic as he explains it in *Reflections in Glass*, how he can assert anything at all. In so strongly asserting the unsearchable transcendence of God without properly balancing this with the immanence of God in the incarnation of the Son, Carnley is left with nowhere to go when he wants to assert truths about the divine.

What we have in *Reflections in Glass*, rather than anything truly orthodox and ancient, is really a religious epistemology which has its roots in the thought of the German Enlightenment philosopher Immanuel Kant (1724–1804). The nineteenth-century theologian H. L. Mansel (1820–1871), on whom Carnley is heavily reliant, was influenced by the deep agnosticism of Kant about knowing ultimate reality. Kant claims that "God" is essentially unknowable. There is however a philosophical query that must be raised with Carnley as it is with Kant: to claim that we cannot know the unknowable appears to presuppose some sort of positive knowledge of the "unknowable." If this were not so, how could the line between what is "unknowable" and what is "knowable" be drawn? Yet draw it Carnley does (following Mansel). I would concur with Carnley if knowing God were only a matter of human efforts from within the phenomenal world to reach out for the transcendent. If, however, there has been an entry into our world from the side of the divine, by a sheer act of grace—a great act of God that is also a meaningful declaration of his sheer love—then we are not guilty of presumption to say that we know God and of God. Christian theology, rightly construed, is merely echoing God's statements about himself.

The archbishop's skepticism about the possibility of human words conveying the truth about God, even when such speech is the gift of revelation, is puzzling given that the word "gospel" itself implies a *verbal* declaration of news from and about God to the world. It is to the implications of this claim—and Broughton Knox's particular exposition of it—that we now turn.

What Broughton Knox Really Said

Peter Carnley is attempting to distinguish his view of revelation from that put forward from Sydney's type of Anglicanism. For Carnley, that view is encapsulated in Broughton Knox's seminal article of 1960.[18] That article now requires a closer examination. What was Knox really saying?

While Donald Robinson was probably the better scholar, Knox, principal of Moore College from 1959–1984, was the master pedagogue, and left his deep imprint on a generation of Sydney clergy and missionaries. This particular article, perhaps his best known single piece, exhibits his characteristic pugilism. He writes specifically against the theologians of midcentury who were speaking about the revelation of God as being an "event" rather than a "word" from God. Many of these were representative of the "Biblical Theology Movement" that was to become quite discredited within a couple of years of the writing of Knox's article.[19] He also names archbishop of Canterbury William Temple (1881–1944) and Leonard Hodgson, Regius Professor of Divinity at the University of Oxford (1889–1969). Scripture was, in the

18. Knox, "Propositional Revelation, the Only Revelation," in *D. Boughton Knox*, 1:307–17.

19. For more on Biblical Theology, see chapter 3.

thought of these scholars, becoming not a means of revelation but a human description of God's great self-revelatory acts in history. In fact, the notion that the "Word of God" as a theological concept involved God speaking was being explicitly denied. God was, for these writers, all action and no talk.

The article, written in Knox's clipped and direct style, addresses this then-fashionable idea that revelation is an *event*, and that the Scriptures merely witness verbally to the revealing event. The Scriptures, according the view Knox contrasts with his own, are not the word of God but are reflections on the deeds of God in which he reveals himself. Not so, asserts Knox; revelation is *propositional*: that is to say, to do with words and the concepts they express. He writes: "Words written meaningfully are, of course, propositions . . . The denial of "propositional revelation" is the denial that God reveals himself to men through the medium of words, that is to say, through meaningful statements and concepts expressed in words, for such is the only sense that can be given to the word "propositional" in this phrase."[20]

Knox defines the term "propositional" *broadly*. In order to explain what he means by "propositional revelation," Knox does not apply a kind of reductive exegesis, distilling unambiguous statements from all kinds of texts; rather he points to the texts themselves including the form in which they appear as propositional, because they are meaningfully verbal. For example, "One of the most important revelations through vision is Daniel's vision of the Son of Man in Daniel 7. Both the vision itself, and the vital interpretation of it, cannot be described otherwise than as "propositional revelation."[21]

Knox did not want to tie the idea of inspiration too closely to the exact words on the page in the manner of the Qur'an. Somehow, the concepts of Scripture are translatable from one language into another and yet still remain revelatory. But Knox did not mean that the narrative or poetic form of the text was therefore merely a shell to be discarded in favor of the kernel of truth contain within it.

As I have already noted, the term "propositional" has often been understood to evoke the philosophical movement labeled "logical positivism." When applied to the idea of scriptural revelation, then, the term "propositional revelation" is understood by some to mean that

20. Knox, *D. Boughton Knox*, 1:307–8.
21. Ibid., 1:311.

Propositional Revelation the Only Revelation?

the narrative or poetic or epistolary *form* of Scripture is irrelevant to the actual meaning that it contains. These matters of genre or structure are merely the wrapping of the content of revelation which needs to be stripped away. In this understanding, "propositions" indicate something like "axioms," or bare statements of literal fact.

Though that is not what Knox or his followers mean by "propositional revelation," it *is* what has been understood by it. Peter Carnley we have cited as one instance of this mistake, and in Humphrey Southern's very critical article we see it repeated.[22] Writing with the tone of a panama-hatted Englishman visiting the benighted and distant colonies, Southern reports that Sydney theology, ". . . starts with a small handful of propositions that are entirely axiomatic and shape with inevitable logic the whole of what follows. Fundamental to this theological method is the understanding that truth—theological truth as much as scientific—can only be expressed in terms of intellectual propositions. Neither narrative nor metaphor nor allegory can convey truth, though they can illustrate it or illuminate it."[23]

As Southern sees it, this leads to a distorted and unbalanced reading of Scripture: "The method also involves strict selectivity in how it allocates authority to Scripture. It is not merely that it affords greater authority to some passages over others, or some biblical writers over others, because of preference: it is the selectivity that says the parables of Jesus, because they are narrative and metaphorical or allegorical, are inherently less capable of informing doctrine than propositions that may (however tendentiously) be drawn from some Pauline writings."[24]

This view would indeed lead to a distorted and unbalanced reading of Scripture if anyone were to hold it. Southern's caricature would be laughable if its effects were not so serious. The view of revelation that Southern here recounts from his journeys in the colonies has never been taught at Moore College and is not now nor is it in evidence in the pulpits of Sydney Anglican churches. Reading beyond the title of Knox's article, it is obvious that this reductionist meaning of the term is not what he meant either.

---

22. Southern, "Anglicanism Sydney Style." The Harrovian Southern is now bishop of Repton, UK.

23. Ibid., 120.

24. Ibid., 122.

But you can see the confusion arising in the use of the term by a friendlier source—principal of Ridley College, Dr. Peter Adam's book *Speaking God's Words*. Adam writes a very enlightening passage about the debate over propositional revelation in which he shows that propositions can be personal and relational and that "propositional" need not be understood to be the opposite of "poetic."[25] He notes, with James Barr, that partly what is at issue here is a description of literary genres and how they operate meaningfully. But at other places in his book, Adam slips back into the more specific use of the word "proposition" to indicate the noetic and conceptual aspect of language as opposed to its affective and aesthetic aspect: "Although biblical revelation includes propositions, however, it also includes many other forms of revelation, such as stories, parables and descriptions of the temple. A biblical doctrine of God's words will certainly include the idea of propositional revelation, but needs to include other categories of revelation as well."[26] Adam goes on to say, "I have tried to show that any view of revelation which is true to the Bible must contain the idea that the Bible includes propositions, but also that it cannot be claimed that revelation is given exclusively in terms of propositions."[27] While Adam's points are well made, the conceptual confusion is scarcely resolved by this slipperiness of usage.

Knox's article is admittedly modest, and it is more than fifty years old. It addressed a particular controversy in theological discourse in polemical style. And there is no question but that Knox overstated his case. Propositional revelation is most certainly *not* the "only revelation"—and Reformed and orthodox evangelicals have never really said that it was. For example, the great Princeton theologian Charles Hodge once wrote: "Nature is as truly a revelation of God as the Bible; and we only interpret the Word of God by the Word of God when we interpret the Bible by science."[28] In this he was merely echoing the entire tradition that follows John Calvin, in fact—the very tradition in which Sydney Anglicans likewise claim to stand. The heat of battle excuses Knox the hyperbole. But greater clarity is needed.

---

25. Adam, *Speaking God's Words*, 91–97.
26. Ibid., 19.
27. Ibid., 96–97.
28. In Noll, *The Scandal of the Evangelical Mind*, 184.

A full-blown monograph on the doctrine of revelation now exists, written by Peter Jensen (1943–), Knox's successor at Moore College.[29] It continues the use of the term "propositional revelation" but clearly does not mean by it what the critics (and some followers) assume it means. As Jensen explains "Christian revelation is basically verbal"[30] in that it conveys both relationship and information. In no way is this idea intended to surpass the affective or aesthetic dimension in the texts of Scripture, as is borne out in the rest of Jensen's book.

Jensen's exposition of the theme of Christian revelation does not deny the reality of divine revelation in the natural world and in human experience. He includes a discussion of the way in which God reveals himself in human experience and in nature but goes on to insist that "it is only through his word that we may truly apprehend his revelation."[31] But it is the gospel of Jesus Christ that is central to his account. The gospel proclamation is the supreme and unsurpassable self-revelation of God to which all other revelation is ordered—the "paradigm or pattern of revelation."[32] And it is hard to escape the inference that this divine self-disclosure is basically *verbal*. The nature of the gospel itself—enclosed in Scripture's words, after all, and described there as a "word of God"—is inescapably verbal. For Jensen "The revelation is not the proper nouns 'Jesus Christ,' but the proposition, 'Jesus is Christ, the Lord.' The divine word comes to us in, and not apart from the words of this gospel."[33]

As we have seen, the false dichotomy, upon which much modern theology unfortunately rests, pits the verbal/propositional against the personal. It was the great emphasis of the Swiss theologian Emil Brunner (1889–1966), for example, that the revelation of God in Jesus Christ was of a person, as opposed to the words and prophecies of the Old Testament. But it isn't a case of either/or: the verbal, or "propositional," is a vehicle for the personal. There is a basic theological mistake in the horror at the thought that a verbal revelation is possible—that human words are too frail to perform as mediums for the divine-human encounter.

---

29. Jensen, *The Revelation of God*. For an extensive appreciative but critical engagement with Jensen, see Myers, "Theologia Evangelii."

30. Jensen, *The Revelation of God*, 87.

31. Ibid., 144.

32. Ibid., 45.

33. Ibid., 49.

If the divine Word became flesh, as the New Testament claims, then surely that divine Word can inhabit words too (John 1:1–18). And that means that words can be both "propositional" (in the sense that they convey information) *and* personal (in that they are the medium of encounter between persons). If words have the power to reveal human beings to one another, it seems entirely unremarkable to suppose that the divine being also reveals himself in this way. Jensen writes, ". . . if the gospel occupies the place in the economy of salvation that its first proponents suggested, and if it accomplishes what they claimed for it, the distinction between personal and propositional knowledge cannot be sustained."[34]

Is the mystery of God in some way compromised by this revelation in speech? The verbal nature of God's revelation does not in fact cramp his freedom; neither does it reduce the wonder and awe with which he is to be beheld by human beings. On the contrary: the revelation of God in the gospel and in Scripture is conveyed with richness and complexity and in such a way as to uphold God's transcendence rather than diminish it.

The Sydney Anglican position on propositional revelation is not eccentric or obscurantist, despite what Southern and Carnley might say. In the field of academic theology, the notion of propositional revelation has made somewhat of a return since the 1990s, as theologians have given greater consideration to the functions and properties of language. For example, the "speech act theory" of the Oxford philosopher J. L. Austin (1911–1960) and others has been adapted by a number of theologians to describe what happens in theological language. Speech act theory has the potential to bridge the divide between revelatory acts and revelatory words and show how the two belong together. The old division between "revelation as event" and "revelation as words" seems now rather happily redundant. In his 1995 work *Divine Discourse*, the Yale philosopher Nicholas Wolterstorff (1932–) defended the notion that God speaks in words.[35] US theologian Kevin J. Vanhoozer (1957–) has been foremost amongst those who have given a fresh description, by means of speech act theory, of the way in which divine words operate.[36]

---

34. Ibid., 88.
35. Wolterstorff, *Divine Discourse*.
36. Vanhoozer, *Is There a Meaning in This Text?*; Vanhoozer, *The Drama of Doctrine*.

God Speaks

What I have tried to demonstrate thus far is that the claim that Christian revelation is "propositional revelation," rightly understood, is neither a novelty nor an antipodean eccentricity. It is entirely within the sphere of orthodox Christian belief to assert that the divine voice is meaningfully heard in verbal form and that the locus of that communication is Holy Scripture. This is not a denial of the experiential or personal aspect of divine revelation. As the well-known UK theologian Alister McGrath (1953–) writes: "To assert that revelation involves information about God is not to deny that it can also involve the mediation of the presence of God, or the transformation of human experience."[37] In fact, it is hard to conceive how a Christian revelation in any proper sense of the word could have no propositional content. What we have observed however, is that the term has been the focus of some confusing debates over the last fifty years or more. Since Knox's feisty article, this debate has affected Sydney Anglicans, like it or not.

The use of particular terminology in any given field is meant to clarify rather than obscure. Terms are only useful as far as they communicate accurately the concepts they signify. When, owing to shifts in culture or context, terminology becomes confusing, it should be abandoned or replaced. I don't think any theologian would dispute that this is especially true in theological discourse. The term "propositional revelation" has certainly caused its fair share of confusion, and seems to be a fair candidate for replacement. If the term is misconstrued and understood too narrowly, then it might be possible for evangelical Christians to become the caricature that Southern describes—to reduce the business of God's revelation of himself to the bare declaration of facts, to which the proper response is merely a kind of cognitive assent.

So, do I have an alternative terminology to suggest? I am attracted to "verbal revelation" as a possible substitute. The obvious criticism of this suggestion is that it is not the words themselves but *what they say* that is the locus of the divine speech, so that the words of God may indeed be translated from one medium, form, or language into another. I would respond that these translated forms—whether sermon, commentary, or a translation of the Bible—derive their status as the word of God from the word of God that they contain.

37. McGrath, *Christian Theology*, 155.

Perhaps there doesn't need to be a replacement term. What this discussion reveals is that a simple word has obscured something that actually needs many words to explain accurately. To insist that God's revelation of himself to human beings is "propositional"—even though that is not all that must be said about it—is to insist on nothing less than that the transcendent and holy God has by his Word through the Holy Spirit meaningfully communicated and today meaningfully communicates with human persons to the end that they might have true and personal knowledge of him, a knowledge that they cannot have without this meaningful self-disclosure. God speaks. Is not that the essence of the Christian gospel? If we say any less do we not deny it altogether?

five

The Romance of Preaching and the Sydney Sermon

A Distinctive Kind of Sermon

People are always picking on the sermon. Not a particular sermon—but the very idea of the sermon. It is, in its own way, notorious—a byword for boredom and irrelevance. But Sydney Anglicans are, if nothing else, the preachers of sermons.

The Sydney Anglican commitment to the authority of Scripture is expressed in what the majority of Sydney Anglican churches do Sunday by Sunday and is reflected in the way in which students are prepared for ministry at Moore College. Or, perhaps this should be stated in reverse: that the central practices of the gathered church are the reading and preaching of the word of God is expressed in the Sydney Anglican commitment to the authority of Scripture. The ministers of the church are trained above all as teachers and preachers of the Bible—with compulsory majors in Old and New Testaments. It is in the activity of preaching the word of God that they count themselves most fulfilling their calling.

And they preach a distinctive *kind* of sermon. They do not pick a particular verse that has come to mind during the week as they have gone about their work. They do not usually follow a set of lectionary readings. Sydney Anglican preachers choose above all things to preach *expository* sermons. The expository sermon is not merely a reflection on Scripture. It is not the kind of sermon that uses a piece of Scripture as a prompt for a discussion of some other topic of the preacher's preference. An expository sermon is a serious attempt to communicate orally what God is saying in the Bible to present day hearers. As Peter Adam from Ridley College said in his 1993 annual Moore College lectures, preaching is "the explanation and application of the Word in the assembled congregation of Christ."[1]

There are threats to the prominence of the sermon in the contemporary Christian world. More pragmatic paradigms of pastoral ministry tend to make the sermon less prominent in the pastor's week. After all, many fine preachers lead small churches. The realization that preaching alone won't fill the church, and the rise of the "celebrity preachers" from the US like John Piper and Mark Driscoll, whose work is freely available online at the click of a mouse, has led to a growing sense of dissatisfaction with the thought that the pastor's chief ministry is to be in the pulpit. Why do Sydney Anglicans preach expository sermons? Will they continue to do so into the future?

The Art of Expository Preaching

Expository sermons are certainly not a novelty in the history of the Christian church. The many extant sermons of John Chrysostom (347–407) and Augustine of Hippo, show that the idea of preaching as explaining a particular text of Scripture is deeply embedded in Christian history. The art of expository preaching was not lost in the Middle Ages, but in the Reformation it was vigorously renewed because of the recaptured emphasis on the supreme authority of Scripture. The great Reformers Martin Luther and John Calvin were preachers above all because of their twofold conviction that the church needed to hear Scripture and submit to it and that Scripture was the vehicle by which the gospel word would come to individual believers. In the Elizabethan era, there were gatherings called "prophesyings" at which ordinary people heard lengthy expositions of Biblical texts while they clutched their Geneva Bibles and took extensive notes. The Puritans of the seventeenth century were renowned for their dedication to biblical preaching. The evangelical movement of the eighteenth century featured church planting and hymn writing, certainly, but above all, it was

---

1. Adam, *Speaking God's Words*, 70.

a *preaching* movement. Its two greatest protagonists were the preachers John Wesley (1703–1791) and George Whitfield (1714–1770).

The preference for expository preaching is based on the conviction that the Bible is the inspired word of God and that to hear the Bible is to hear the voice of God himself. The expository sermon thus has the grand, even heroic, task of mediating the divine voice to the present-day hearer. Phillip Jensen (1945–), the present Dean of Sydney, explains that this form of preaching, "means saying what God did say when he was here on earth in the person of his Son. It means saying what God has said, and continues to say, through the inspired Scripture. True preaching is preaching that unfolds and explicates and explains and declares the living and active words of God."[2] Like no other human activity, preaching Scripture mediates the presence of God. Since Scripture is God's word, to preach Scripture is to invite the Holy Spirit to do his work in and around that word. It invites the possibility that God will transform those who hear. Donald Robinson's conviction was that "preaching is . . . directly related to God's method or methods of bringing men to salvation."[3]

John Stott and the Expository Sermon in Sydney

The rise of the expository sermon model in Sydney Anglican churches received particular impetus from the visit of the great English preacher John Stott (1922–2011) to Sydney in 1958. Well-known local evangelist John Chapman reportedly said that he tore up his old sermons once he had heard Stott preach! Stott's sermons were models of engagement with the text in its context. The passages selected were long enough to show that the meaning of the text was not being distorted. The preacher, after a few introductory remarks, works his or her way methodically and unemotionally through the passage, teasing out its logic and explaining to the congregation how its logic fits together. The text is then applied to the hearers, ideally, on the basis of what has been gleaned from this close examination. The sermon will usually form part of a series on a particular book of the Bible or part of the Bible.

---

2. Jensen and Grimmond, *The Archer and the Arrow*, 19.
3. Robinson, *Donald Robinson*, 2:136.

Stott distilled his theory of preaching in a 1982 book, *I Believe in Preaching*,[4] contending that all true Christian preaching is expository preaching. He went on to clarify what this meant:

> Of course if by an "expository" sermon is meant a verse-by-verse explanation of a lengthy passage of Scripture, then indeed it is only one possible way of preaching, but this would be to misuse the word. Properly speaking, "exposition" has a much broader meaning. It refers to the content of the sermon (biblical truth) rather than its style (a running commentary). To expound Scripture is to bring out of the text what is there and expose it to view.[5]

That may be so; but Stott himself was master of the "running commentary" style of expository preaching. He preached immaculately prepared sermons with an English coolness of manner that were, in their way, aesthetically pleasing in their plainness of style and reserve of emotion and in their directedness towards their purpose—a bit like modernist architecture, all clean lines and balance. He may have said: "The size of the text is immaterial, so long as it is biblical. What matters is what we do with it," but on the whole his sermons were on texts of a regular size, a few verses long.

For Stott the expository nature of the sermon sets limits within which the preacher can effectively and meaningfully work. It gives boundaries to the preacher and prevents him or her from straying into the mere giving of opinions. That the task of the preacher is expositional gives great confidence to him or her because of the conviction that Scripture is God's word: "If we were expatiating upon our own views or those of some fallible fellow human being, we would be bound to do so diffidently. But if we are expounding God's Word with integrity and honesty, we can be very bold."[6]

Stott's emphasis on expository preaching reveals a commitment to a certain way of doing theological thinking. The exegesis of the text that should be the foundation of proper expository preaching is to be "a discipline of the utmost rigor." The Reformers of the sixteenth century had emphasized the "plain" or "literal" meaning of the text over against the fanciful allegories that were a feature of medieval expositions. This

---

4. Stott, *I Believe in Preaching*.
5. Ibid., 125–6.
6. Ibid., 132.

"plain" meaning is the preacher's task to expound—a task that is not always straightforward. The Reformers were likewise committed to the unity of the Scriptures, such that it should be allowed to "interpret itself." That is, as article 20 of the *Thirty-Nine Articles of the Church of England* (1572) states, the preacher is not free to "expound one place of Scripture that it be repugnant to another."

Stott's method works brilliantly on the epistles of Paul and it displays all the strengths—and weaknesses—of English evangelicalism as opposed to its American cousin. The claim is that it is a prisoner to no grand theological system. It is not interested in squeezing a text into a preconceived confession. It is interested in what *this* text says to us here today. It is a commitment to let all the parts of Scripture speaks in their own voice. This decision by those who stand in pulpits has shaped theological thinking: while Sydney Anglicans will describe themselves as Calvinist and Reformed, they are by and large not *that* Reformed—especially compared to some American Calvinists. Broughton Knox wrote against limited atonement—a touchstone of Calvinist orthodoxy for some. This is because, as he said, "it is a doctrine without a text."[7] And that, for Knox, was that! Likewise, he was doubtful about the doctrine of the imputation of Christ's righteousness, which sits of very slim textual foundations if at all. This is an approach to theology driven primarily from the preacher's point of view.

The danger for Stott's preaching was that it became atomistic. It was perhaps better at explaining the parts than relating the parts to the whole. This is where Biblical Theology has been a great asset to preaching, because it enables the preacher to show how each text both speaks with its own voice *and* contributes to the whole of the Bible's message.

But the reduced emphasis on the great confessions of the Christian faith and on the possibility of a system of Christian doctrine presents a new danger for Sydney Anglican preachers and their congregations. Under God, proper preaching depends on the commitment of the preacher to ex-posit and ex-egete the text. Preachers have to imagine, for a moment at least, that they can divest themselves from all presuppositions and prior commitments. This is not a mistake—in all kinds of disciplines we need to at least aim at objectivity, even though this is not quite possible. The pitfall to avoid is when you imagine that pure presupposition-less objectivity is actually achievable and you deny that

---

7. "Some Aspects of the Atonement," in *Broughton Knox*, 1:236.

you have prior commitments or theological convictions that shape your reading of the text. Inevitably, this means that the sermon is constantly filled with poor and unreflected-upon theological assumptions and assertions. That is: *expository* preaching depends upon the preacher's determination to submit to the text and not impose upon it. But if they imagine that they brings no theological presuppositions to the text, they are merely in denial. They will, in fact, be a poor and unreflective and *untheological* reader of the text in question. They will not build and repair their systematic theology if they deny that they have one in the first place. And they will certainly not exegete the text well, either. As Phillip Jensen writes, "As faithful preachers we must put aside the illusion that we are unpolluted sponges, ready to soak up God's word and squeeze it out, pure and fresh, for our adoring listeners. We must work hard at shaping our own systematic and biblical theology in the light of what God actually says. Good preachers must be good biblical and systematic theologians."[8]

The Preacher as Heroic Figure

Preaching is carried out by preachers. Although as Protestants, Sydney Anglican evangelicals do not have a priestly view of the ministry, preachers are certainly designated, called, and highly trained for their role. For all the talk about every-member ministry, it is preaching that is the chief ministry in the congregation and the most special calling. The figure of the preacher assumes an almost heroic status. Ideally, the preacher imitates Christ himself—and like one of the great martyrs of the church, is ready to suffer for the truth if necessary. Actually, it would be more accurate to say that the preacher imitates the apostle Paul as he in turn speaks of his own imitation of Christ in his ministry in 1 and 2 Corinthians. The onerous duty of preachers is that they are called upon to say hard as well as gentle things; but this risky duty lends to the preaching profession a sense of romance.

The preacher's privilege is extraordinary. Their ministry is not merely in God's service; it is in the terrifying honor of being God's mouthpiece. The ministry of the word is the first and most important of ministries, and they are its designated exponent for the congregation.

---

8. Jensen and Grimmond, *The Archer and the Arrow*, 66.

The word of God *constitutes* the church in its very essence. It calls it into being. And the preacher wields this word—not exclusively or without accountability, but as their calling and duty.

If being a preacher is a joy with many delights, then it is also a burden with many pains. The dramatization of the role of the preacher in the life of the congregation is reflected in Phillip Jensen's description of the preaching profession as "inherently dangerous."[9] As he puts it. "If we are going to be faithful preachers of the very words of God, delivering, explaining and applying his message to the people he has given us to love, we need to be ready for those times when people don't love us back . . . This sort of faithfulness will inevitably lead to difficulty, conflict, suffering and persecution."[10]

The heroism of expository preaching in Sydney has been further shaped by the Katoomba Christian Conventions. The KCC is a nondenominational organization with evangelical convictions, but Sydney Anglicans have had a substantial influence in it and have been substantially influenced by it. The conventions, especially the Youth Convention which ran from the 1970s until the mid-2000s in January each year, are intended to be a showcase of the best preachers and the best preaching.[11] Though the KCC is nondenominational, Sydney Anglicans were often on the platform.[12] It is the occasional nature and remarkable setting of the convention that means that the preaching heard there lingers long in the memory in a way in which the regular Sunday preaching tends not to.

At Katoomba, preachers like John Chapman, John Woodhouse, and Phillip Jensen ministered to thousands of people in their late teens and early adulthood. Those who would fill Moore College to overflowing in the 1990s and 2000s had filled Katoomba's massive tent in 1980s. It would be very difficult to forget Woodhouse's remarkable exposition of the book of Leviticus in 1986 as a model of what could be done with

9. Ibid., 107.

10. Ibid., 114–5.

11. The Katoomba Youth Convention as such is now defunct but several other conventions run in its place.

12. A quick count of speakers at the youth convention from 1978–2006 reveals that more than 75 percent of them were Sydney Anglicans. Of the rest, a number were Presbyterians or Baptists who had trained at Moore College. See http://shop.kcc.org.au/cubecart/index.php?act=viewCat&catId=8.

the Sydney Anglican method of preaching. Leviticus is perhaps the least promising of all Old Testament books for a sermon series—and especially for a series at a major conference at which the organizers were hoping to attract thousands of young people. And yet, without resorting to a terrible and bizarre legalism, Woodhouse preached this difficult text as God's word for Christian believers today—as gospel, in other words.

At the same time, Phillip Jensen's ministry at the University of New South Wales was rapidly expanding. Jensen knew the Stott method, but he also knew his Biblical Theology. He was a penetrating social critic, had read widely, and was not afraid to negate what was false as well as to affirm what was true. It was a heady mix. His mid-week campus Bible study at the university was filled to overflowing with students twice a week and sometimes more. He was capable of speaking for a complete lunch hour without losing his mostly teenage audience. The backbone of Jensen's preaching was (and is) prayerful hard work with the text of Scripture. This kept his preaching fresh, because he was not merely dependent on his own opinions week by week. With sometimes abstruse but dazzling argument, he took his listeners into the world of the Bible so that they might hear the voice of God himself. While at times disavowing emotion—especially when critiquing charismatic theology—and keenly aware of the potential for his rhetoric to become merely manipulative, Jensen was also a powerfully emotive speaker. He did not fail to miss the affective aspect of the word of God, and he felt compelled to convey it. His preaching was polemical and dramatic, and it transformed many, many lives. Here was preaching that did what preachers had long claimed preaching could do, under God.

Among overseas speakers, Professor Don Carson from Trinity Evangelical Divinity School consistently modeled a form of expository preaching that was compelling in a number of directions—intellectually stimulating *and* spiritually satisfying. Carson traveled to the preaching platforms of Sydney on numerous occasions, but perhaps most memorably when he spoke on Paul's prayers—material that would later become his *A Call to Spiritual Reformation*.[13] That Carson is a Baptist is of no concern to Sydney Anglicans, who see him as a fellow traveler and a leader among the world's evangelicals.

---

13. Carson, *A Call to Spiritual Reformation*.

Though it is something of a habit to bemoan the standard of preaching, the quality of preaching in ordinary Sydney pulpits is very high.[14] The overwhelming majority of preachers are well-trained (often to postgraduate level), mature, and articulate. Even so, there were, for a couple of decades, a small group of local preachers who exemplified what expository preaching could achieve, and whose leadership of the movement as a whole was linked to their presence in the pulpit. Phillip Jensen's influence was increased by the recording, cataloging, and distribution of tapes of his sermons. After the turn of the millennium, however, this technology was swiftly and rapidly superseded by the advent of mp3s and the Internet. It became possible to hear the best of overseas preachers like John Piper, Mark Driscoll, and Tim Keller regularly, and almost without cost. Each of these men, whose Reformed convictions Sydney Anglicans share, has built enormous ministries in large US cities on a scale unimaginable in Australia. Preachers now preach in an environment where truly extraordinary preaching is available to their congregations in a few quick mouse-clicks.

I have spoken here about the dramatization of the role of the preacher in the culture of evangelicalism. To point it out is not to deride it. I think this dramatization is entirely appropriate in a church or fellowship of churches that wants to be a church that listens to the word of God as its focal point. Where it becomes problematic is when the expectation that there will be rejection and persecution for preachers leads to a deafness to genuinely constructive criticism. The preacher speaks the words of God but does so as a fallible and sinful human being. The word that is spoken is a human word as well as a word of God. Sometimes preachers will be simply inept; at other times, they will be mistaken. They may be confused and inarticulate. They may be in sinful error. To point out any of these, a person should not be made to feel as if they are being directly disobedient to the word of God, or stoking the flames beneath a martyr's pyre. It seriously dishonors the memory of the genuine martyrs to call a little bit of robust disagreement "persecution" and "rejection." In fact, what is needed is a clarification of in what

---

14. Of course this is a matter of opinion! However, I recently spoke to one parish nominator who had listened to forty or more different local preachers in their search for a new rector and they were impressed by the coherence, scriptural faithfulness, and applicability of the sermons they heard.

sense if any preaching should be held to be the word of God. To that matter we now turn.

Is Preaching the Word of God?

How does preaching relate to the notion of the word of God? Is it itself the word of God? Peter Adam addressed this very question in his Moore College lectures.[15] He notes how the issue was raised in the Second Helvetic Confession of 1566 that states that "the preaching of the Word of God is the Word of God." From statements like this it has often been assumed that the Protestant Reformers equated preaching with the word of God quite directly. For example, Adam notes that this statement—which is actually in the marginalia of the Confession—has been taken as a Reformation axiom by Klaas Runia (1926–2006) and Donald Bloesch (1928–2010) and other recent evangelical writers. However, Adam suggests that the concept needs more careful theological treatment. He looks at Heinrich Bullinger's sermons—since Bullinger (1504–1575) was the author the aforementioned confession it seems worth asking what Bullinger might have thought he meant. Adam asserts that Bullinger was arguing that "sermons are the means by which the Word of God is applied to people, not that the preaching of the Word of God is the Word of God"[16] in the baldest sense. In the verse usually used to support a closer identification of preaching and the word of God—1 Thessalonians 2:13—Paul seems to be speaking about his particular authority as an apostle rather than his more general role as a preacher.[17] Adam deduces: "it may be fair to infer that when we preach Paul's words we are preaching the Word of God, but it does not necessarily follow that our preaching is in itself the Word of God."[18]

For Adam, too high a view of preaching as the word of God may cause problems because it may herald the beginning of a Protestant papacy. Too close an identification of the preacher's human words with "the word of God" gives the preaching itself unwarranted and apparently underived authority. Preaching is authoritative and divinely

15. Adam, *Speaking God's Words*, 112ff.

16. Ibid., 115.

17. I notice that he doesn't discuss 1 Peter 4:11: "If anyone speaks, let him speak as one speaking the oracles of God."

18. Adam, *Speaking God's Words*, 115.

inspired (we might say) and ought to be received as such inasmuch as it is derived from and faithful to the divinely inspired text. We should speak of "preaching the word of God"—with Scripture remaining the word of God that is so preached—rather than preaching *being in some independent way* the word of God.

Adam writes:

> Perhaps the best way of describing it is to say that when human beings explain the Word of God, preach it, teach it, and urge people to accept it, then the Word of God achieves its purpose and this is one of the normal ways in which God brings his Word to human beings. It is perhaps helpful to describe this in terms of the work of the Spirit... The Scripture itself is a product of the Spirit, and when the Spirit works in the preacher and in the hearers, the words of God are mediated and bear fruit in the lives of those who hear.[19]

Persecution and trouble will still come to the faithful preacher. Theirs is still a "romantic" calling. But because we make that necessary distinction between the word of God in Scripture and the word of God as it is delivered by preachers, we avoid elevating preachers themselves above contradiction—a dizzying altitude whose thin air is not for human beings. For Peter Adam, "if our preaching is true to Scripture it will be the means by which God brings the Word of God to those who hear us." Thus we can speak, I think, of preaching *as* the word of God when it is preaching *of* the word of God. The drama of the preacher's calling remains in that they have to wrestle against flesh and blood to be as faithful to the word of God written as they can possibly be, in service of the church.

The Confusion of Terms

The notion of preaching as it has come to be understood and practiced in evangelical pulpits is beset by terminological and theological confusions. Peter Adam, as we have already seen, defines preaching as "the explanation and application of the Word in the assembled congregation of Christ."[20] That definition certainly reflects current practice. Yet it is hard to find a direct comparison between what we can see practiced in

19. Ibid., 118.
20. Ibid., 70.

the New Testament—and the terminology that was used to describe it—and what we know as "preaching" in the churches of the Sydney diocese and elsewhere. There is certainly a well-established *tradition* of preaching as a sustained expository monologue from a trained pastor in the setting of a church service. This tradition may be an authentic development from the New Testament experience, but it is hard to see how it directly compares to what happened in the early churches.

Characteristically, Donald Robinson worked on the words. In an unpublished paper read at the Autumn School of Theology held at Moore College in 1966, Robinson pointed out that there are three fairly clearly distinct activities by which the word of God is conveyed in the New Testament. There is the handing on, or teaching, of the *paradosis* or tradition. There was the activity of prophecy, a highly valued gift in which exhortations and encouragements were delivered. And then there was the preaching of the gospel to those outside the church: "the very spearhead of God's overture to lost mankind."[21]

The conventional "sermon" (from the Greek, "a word") is usually a mixture of all three of these things in various proportions. A preacher characteristically preaches the gospel, passes on the faith "once delivered to all the saints," and prophesies (in the sense that Donald Robinson means it here). Yet it would also be the case that these activities are not restricted to formal occasions. The ministry of the word, Sydney Anglicans would want to emphasize, can take place mutually and informally. Those without office in the church are invited to join in this mutual word ministry. Romans 15:14 calls on Christians to "instruct one another" and is confident of the capability of any Christian in the Spirit to perform this role. The day of Pentecost, after all, was declared by Peter to by the fulfillment of the prophecy of Joel that the Spirit would be poured out on young men and women such that prophecy would no longer be a gift restricted to a few carefully designated individuals. Phillip Jensen wants to use the terminology of "preaching" to describe these activities as well—in order to democratize them and to encourage them. This would represent a different use of the term "preaching" than that deployed by Robinson and Adam.[22]

While there is a kind of democratization of this ministry of the word, there is also in practice the sense in which "preaching" is

21. Robinson, *Donald Robinson*, 2:144.
22. Adam, *Speaking God's Words*, 120.

connected to a particular "office" and is the work of a particular designated individual, the preacher. The sermon that is preached by this person is usually given the bulk of the time in a church service. It is somewhat confusing to use "preaching" language to describe the informal encouragements and exhortations that occur between Christians. Furthermore, there is no need for a sense of embarrassment that giving this particular person's word ministry pride of place contradicts the Reformation notion of "priesthood of all believers." Far better to use the label "ministry of the word" to describe that general activity and to reserve "preaching" for the specific, formal monologue in the church meeting.

It is extremely useful to have the terminology of the New Testament clarified and shown that it doesn't quite fit with today's practice of preaching. This helps us to be appropriately flexible about our customs. But it is entirely appropriate that this traditional practice has developed as a way of receiving the New Testament material rather than as a way of expressing it exactly. Returning to the primitive terminology in order to clear away the accretions of traditional practice, as if in that terminology was indicator of an underlying and original normativity, is a dubious process. It is doubtful whether a completely coherent or consistent answer could be found. The New Testament terminology is somewhat loose and overlapping. The data is too sketchy. Enormous effort has been put into trying to define what "prophecy" and "teaching" and "preaching" actually mean, on the assumption that the usage of these terms by the New Testament church reflects a normative practice. I not at all convinced that this is a productive line of inquiry. "Preaching" as we know it now is an activity of the church that is entirely in keeping with the kind of church it has learned to be from reading the New Testament—even if it turns out that it is not exactly what the churches of the New Testament were doing when they met.

Preach the Word

In an essay responding to the work of Donald Robinson, Ben Underwood has written, "'Preach the word' (1 Tim 4:2) is not so much an exhortation to make Biblical exposition the method of our preaching; rather it is an exhortation to make the gospel of Christ the substance of our preaching."²³ Yet it is because of the form in which the gospel of Christ comes to us that Biblical exposition has become the consistent method used for teaching and exhorting God's people from the pulpit in Sydney. Exposition of the Bible enables the speaker to keep the message of Jesus Christ, crucified and risen, at the forefront, since that is what the Bible is about.

The temptation is of course to preach some other content because it is more nakedly practical and relevant. Congregations are yearning for preaching that is connected to their everyday lives. But the Bible is not a self-help manual or a handbook for living. What is required of preachers, then, is not the terrible slide into relevance, or its opposite— a kind of deliberate, purist disconnection. As long ago as 1966, Robinson wrote, "one of our big weaknesses is in what is called 'application' in imparting God's Word. I don't mean a personal appeal tacked on to the end of a sermon. I mean an awareness on the part of the speaker of the condition of the audience, and the addressing of the utterance to that particular condition . . . In prophecy, at least, it is not enough to pass on what God has shown to me. It is to pass on what God has revealed to me for your edification or encouragement."²⁴ He went on: "a chief defect of modern preaching is that it is so often fundamentally impersonal: no amount of earnestness, or desire to get decisions, or shouting, or belaboring the audience, or tricks of rhetoric, of even conversational tone, will make up for a lack of awareness on the speaker's part of just who he is talking to, and what their spiritual condition is in the actuality of their daily lives, and what they are likely to make of what he says . . . Too many sermons, if they terminate anywhere, terminate on themselves."²⁵

The same complaint might be made in the twenty-first century. Sermons are not adorned by relevance *per se*. But they are addressed to real people. The preacher's task is incomplete if he is not also a shepherd of the flock whom God has given him to love.

It is because preaching concerns the word of the true God to real people that a reinvigoration of preaching will not centrally be a focus on a technique or method but on the development of a heart for God and for people. It is not completely a mistake to study preaching itself. But the preacher must primarily study to love God and to love his people. If

---

23. Ben Underwood, "Preaching the Word," in *Donald Robinson*, 3:191.
24. Robinson, *Donald Robinson*, 2:146–7.
25. Ibid., 147.

Sydney Anglican preaching has ever been anything of note in the world, it has been when and where its exponents have been filled with these twin loves.

Part Two:

The Church

six

"Wherever Two or Three are Gathered": The Knox-Robinson Doctrine of the Church

Evangelicals and the Church

Evangelical Protestantism is by definition a rejection of an overblown view of the church. Because of the ease with which they cooperate across denominational barriers, it has often been said that evangelicals *have* no doctrine of the church, or "ecclesiology." Certainly, the great statements of faith of the evangelical missionary societies and student movements tend not to make particular claims about church. Partly this is because they aren't themselves "churches," of course, but the result is that evangelicals appear to hold ecclesiological matters to be of a secondary importance.

But the impression that evangelicals have no ecclesiology is not at all accurate. For their part, Sydney Anglicans have indeed given an enormous amount of attention to the doctrine of the church in their writings since the 1950s. Other evangelicals may have been able to remain somewhat agnostic on ecclesiological matters. For the evangelical Anglicans in the diocese of Sydney, the debates over the formation of the national Anglican Church in Australia and the rise of the ecumenical movement have together been a forge in which an evangelical doctrine of the church has taken shape. This view of church has become known as the "Knox-Robinson" view of the church because it owes its existence to the work of Donald Robinson and Broughton Knox.[1]

This ecclesiology has caused the utmost bewilderment and irritation among Sydney's critics, especially the Anglican ones. The purpose of this chapter is to chart the rise of the "Knox-Robinson" view of the church and to evaluate it. There have been real gains for Sydney Anglicans in holding to the ecclesiology that they do. But it is also fair to say that there are some problematic consequences that need to be properly scrutinized.

Where Is the Church?

Though Anglicans may affirm in the creeds that the church is "one," to be Anglican is to reckon with a plurality of institutions called "church" in the world. You cannot be a member of the church that almost *per definition* is divided from the Church of Rome and assert that the essential unity of the church is in its institutional structures. Clearly, the Church of England has in its DNA the knowledge that not only is there a Roman church from which she has separated but also that other nations may indeed have their own churches. It is a fundamental component of Anglican ecclesiology that the Church of England is not the only church on earth.

Having said that, Anglicans and others have often used the language of "the church" as if they were the universal church on earth—the "general" church. As the British Empire grew in the nineteenth century, and the Church of England itself began to look more and more global, this habit of speech assumed almost triumphalist proportions. The emergence and near-complete triumph of Anglo-Catholicism in that era also saw a new emphasis among Anglicans on their ecclesiological wholeness. The volume was certainly turned up on matters ecclesiological. Evangelical Anglicans, who have a characteristic distaste for the formalism and rigidity of institutional Christianity, seemed out of kilter within their own native church structures. Often they had nothing to say in response to the increasingly bold claims made for ecclesiology by their Anglo-Catholic co-religionists. They preferred to operate on the

---

1. As we shall see, the term is somewhat of a misnomer since Knox and Robinson held different views on some aspects of the doctrine of the church. What they had in common was the emphasis on the local.

boundaries of the organization called "the church," cooperating with other, non-Anglican evangelicals in mission and in charity.

By the middle of the twentieth century, we could point to another factor too. The rise of the ecumenical movement in the 1930s was always a cause of puzzlement to evangelicals, who had long been used to interdenominational cooperation and who did not feel the need to attend lengthy and expensive conferences exploring how ecumenical cooperation might be possible. For them it already was. Having said that, evangelicals had a clear sense of which church groups they could and could not work with and were simply less interested in talking through differences with those they felt sure they could not work with. The ecumenical movement, however, was making quite specific claims about the nature of "the church" and the need for its institutional union as a fulfillment of its divinely-given purpose.

The claims made for "church" by fellow Anglicans and by the ecumenical movement were an invitation to evangelical Anglicans in Sydney in the 1950s to think about the nature and essence of the church. The World Council of Churches, established in 1948, met in Evanston, Canada in 1954 and in New Delhi in 1961. The National Conference of Australian Churches met in Melbourne in 1960. The Church of England in Australia was at the same time pressing towards the development of its own constitution that would be finalized in 1961. Were these entities really "church"?

Robinson and Knox

Donald Robinson had already been prepared for these challenges by his studies at Cambridge in the 1940s, where almost by accident he took an intensive course of study on the theme of the church. It was also his linguistic skills which were to open the way to an insight about ecclesiology that was to prove determinative. In his early study, Robinson learned of the possibility for confusion that comes when one speaks of "the doctrine of the church." The English term "church," which is used to translate the Greek New Testament word *ekklesia* implies in its ordinary English usage something institutional and structural. The original use of the word *ekklesia* did not however mean anything of the kind. It simply meant "gathering" or "assembly." The "doctrine of the church" was not at all the same as the meaning of the word usually translated church. That wasn't to say there was no connection, but only that there was certainly a large potential for grave confusion.

We have already noted the leading role that Robinson took in the development of Biblical Theology at Moore College. But of course he was also an expert linguist and a creative exegete, committed to the view that the text of Scripture needed to speak for itself in the parts as well as in the whole. He had enormous faith that dealing with the words on the page at a micro-level would deliver results. Even though he had taken on board James Barr's sweeping criticism of the linguistic and semantic methods of the Biblical Theologians in the 1950s, it was still the case that his approach to a particular issue might be to enquire after the usage of the term in the New Testament. He recalls the influence of the Sydney University philologist G. P. Shipp:

> From Shipp I learned a little about how to assess the actual semantic value of words as they are used by individual writers and in particular contexts, without simply importing a dictionary meaning into them with a heavy hand. I began to find a Greek concordance of more use than a lexicon: the lexicon tells you what a word might mean, while the concordance encourages you to consider how it is actually used. Even with the small instinct for semantics that I had acquired, I began, in my theological studies, to discover that many commentators and theologians tended to read more into the meanings of words than either context or usage warranted, and did not allow for subtle changes of meaning of words from one writer to another or even from one context to another in the same writer. My own first published efforts were semantic-studies.[2]

Robinson would often be criticized for his reliance on linguistic analysis of individual words—especially in his study of the doctrine of the church. This was unfair. But it was certainly true that he grasped the necessity of dealing with words as they actually appear and of disciplining theological thought by reference to the words of Scripture. Too often, he observed, the word "church" was being used to describe entities and institutions that were not, in New Testament terms at least (and what other terms matter?), "church." As he wrote: "There is no greater source of confusion in our speaking about the church today than the practice of using 'church' to mean the organized structures built up to

---

2. Robinson, *Donald Robinson*, 1:262.

ensure the continuance of a formal Christianity, and to show a certain face to the world. To call this social structure 'the church' might be a mere linguistic shift of no great importance, were it not that theological claims are made for this 'organization church' which biblically belong to an altogether different 'church.'"[3]

This would certainly not do. As early as 1951, having satisfied himself that the New Testament usage of *ekklesia* referred almost exclusively to the local church, Robinson began formulating a theology of the church which took its start from the epistle to the Ephesians and from the related but not identical concept of the church in Hebrews.

In his article on "Church" in the evangelical *New Bible Dictionary* Robinson claims that no writer in the NT uses *ekklesia* in the collective way to speak of the congregations as a whole. An *ekklesia* is a meeting or assembly—most commonly an assembly of citizens. Robinson argues that in Acts, James, 3 John, Revelation, and in the earlier Paulines *ekklesia* is "always a particular local congregation." In Colossians and Ephesians, Paul "generalizes his use of 'church' to indicate, not an ecumenical church, but the spiritual and heavenly significance of each and every local 'body' which has Christ as its 'head,' and by which God demonstrates his manifold wisdom through the creation of 'one new man' out of all races and classes.'"[4]

Then comes a characteristic move. Robinson claims that the New Testament describes the one church as gathered in the heavenly realm. The earthly church is pluriform—it gives expression to the heavenly church as it gathers. The heavenly church is uniform and continuous. The earthly church is intermittent and localized. He writes: "Church" is not a synonym for the "people of God"; it is rather an *activity* of the "people of God."[5] He goes on "the church is a *meeting* under the headship of Christ; in its meeting it is *a body*; as a body it is *one*. It follows that he who is not in the meeting is not in the body."[6]

Thus for Robinson, "church" is more of a verb than a noun. "Church" fundamentally involves actual "churching"—that is, *gathering*. This means that the church exists in two basic ways in the present time. It is a heavenly gathering around the ascended Lord that is

3. Ibid., 1:236–7.
4. Ibid., 1:222–3.
5. Ibid., 1:223.
6. Ibid.

a "continuous assembly," and it is manifested in local assemblies of believers that "come and go"—they are intermittently "church."[7] In Robinson's view, there is no sense in which "church" can be used to describe an aggregate of believers. He writes: "It is not too much to say that the church on earth does not exist, or is not visible, except in the actual assembly of believers."[8] The continuously gathered heavenly church is (as Robinson's student Peter O'Brien would later say) *manifested* in the local gatherings of believers.[9]

The two passages of Scripture that were crucial for this observation were Ephesians 2:6 and Hebrews 12:22–24. In Ephesians 2:6 we read of the believers being raised up and "seated in the heavenly realms with Christ Jesus." In Hebrews 12:22–24, the author uses the perfect tense to describe how the believers have already come to the "heavenly Jerusalem, the city of the living God" and to "thousands upon thousands of angels in joyful assembly, to the *ekklesia* of the firstborn." These two very dramatic and vivid passages speak of the security of the church in its present heavenly gathering, which becomes in both instances the ground for a great confidence and hope. The scattered and persecuted local gatherings can look then to this heavenly and universal entity for their assurance.

In Robinson's view, there is no place, therefore, for a concept of the "general" or "universal" church, since it cannot gather. If the church does not meet, it is not a church. If the word "church" is applied to non-gathering entities, the significance of the local church as *the* church will likely be obscured. And yet Paul can address his letters to a particular local church to "the church of God in Corinth"—as if it is totally and sufficiently "church" without reference to a greater earthly entity called "church."

There are three intriguing consequences for ecclesiology that flow from this observation about the way "church" is used in the New Testament. The first is that the unity of the church is not to be found in the institutional arrangements of the earthly church but in the gospel of Jesus Christ. Robinson wrote, "Of the life and organization of the

---

7. Ibid., 1:236.

8. Ibid.

9. "The local congregations or house-groups are earthly manifestations of that heavenly assembly gather around God and Christ" (O'Brien, "The Church as a Heavenly and Eschatological Entity," 97).

churches generally, we know very little, except for Jerusalem, which was not typical. Yet what we know makes us confident that their unity lay in the gospel itself, acceptance of the OT Scriptures and acknowledgement of Jesus as "Lord and Christ."[10] The church is not unified because of obedience to a particular form of ministry, because of its celebration of the Lord's Supper, or because it has a shared hierarchical structure. It is unified quite without and before those things, in the gospel of Jesus Christ, its holy Lord. Its unity is established by him and is a heavenly, rather than an earthly reality. What's more, the local church is described in ways that indicate that it, like the heavenly church, is a complete entity, lacking for nothing to make it fully "church." This means that quests for the earthly, organizational unity of the church are quite misplaced if they overlook the necessity for agreement in the gospel. No group of bishops sharing cups of tea and shuffling papers is going to unify the church. After all, it is not their gathering on earth that constitutes them as a "church". Rather it is their gathering in heaven around Christ that leads them to form local earthly communal associations. Broughton Knox also emphases this theme: "Denominations are not churches, but are service structures to assist congregations which are real churches."[11]

Thus, according to the Knox-Robinson view, the national Anglican Church of Australia is somewhat misnamed. It is not a "church" in the sense that it never gathers. It is more properly described as a fellowship of churches. It cannot assume for itself the theological concept of "church," or use that language to leverage itself over and against the local church. It ought not to speak of itself with reference to the "body of Christ" and "temple" metaphors—it does violence to those theological concepts when it does so. Knox wrote, "these patterns of fellowship beyond local gatherings take the form, in our time, of denominations, which, regrettably instead of being aids to fellowship, have become restrictive of fellowship. What we need to do is to recognize the unessential character of the denominational links and to modify them where they interfere with fellowship and where they are inclined to restrict fellowship to within the denomination itself."[12] The denomination cannot speak of its unity as being the same as the New Testament concept

---

10. Robinson, *Donald Robinson*, 1:229.
11. Knox, *D. Broughton Knox*, 2:36.
12. Ibid., 2:31.

of the unity of the church and so seek to coerce its members to be in unity with it in the name of the true unity of the church.

The ramifications of this understanding of "church" over against "denomination" are ongoing in the life of the national Anglican Church. Archbishop Peter Jensen expressed it this way in his address to Sydney synod in 2011:

> Sydney always insisted that the national federation be decentralized in ethos and diocesan in structure as it is under the Constitution . . . We think of the Constitution as a compact, an agreement between Australian Anglicans to behave within certain boundaries and where possible to leave each other to get on with local initiatives to defend and promote the gospel. The national church is best served when the decentralized, diocesan-focused constitution is observed in fact and in spirit. In our federation, it is the dioceses which matter most, just as in the diocese it is the parishes which matter most.[13]

Much of the tension between Sydney and other dioceses in the Anglican Church of Australia can be explained in terms of a difference of opinion about centralism over federalism. Even within the Sydney diocese itself, there remains a tension between the principle of the priority of the local expression of church in the parish and the demands of the diocese itself.

The second consequence is that the earthly, local gathering cannot be said to have a mission. Evangelism is not, strictly speaking, a purpose for which the church exists, according to Robinson. The church is a gathering of believers whose focus is inwards and upwards but not outwards.[14] Being an action and not a thing, the church cannot have some function other than the assembling of God's people. Robinson wrote:

> The church has no such task or role. *Christians* do; and the *only* those Christians who in their particular callings are at work in these places. I cannot think of anything in the New Testament which suggests that the church . . . or even Christians as a visibly organized body, have a function of witness or service vis-à-vis the world. Christians should think of themselves in the world, not as the church, but as God's people, set among the nations to show forth His excellencies by the character of their good

13. Peter Jensen, "Presidential Address."
14. O'Brien, "The Church as a Heavenly and Eschatological Entity," 114.

works, and by any special ministry that may have been committed to each. But in their appearance it is not that of a church or congregation but of a dispersion; they seem not a "kingdom of priests" but "strangers and pilgrims"; men see not their corporate "worship" but their individual "good works"; and their unity in such witness and service will be manifested only in "the day of visitation."[15]

The New Testament focus is on the relationships and responsibilities that the members of the body of Christ have to Christ and to each other. This is not a denial of the necessity for missionary activity. On the contrary: it is a description of the church as the purpose of the mission rather than the instrument of it. Individual Christians have the task of evangelism, not some entity we might call "church."[16]

Third, for Broughton Knox it was "fellowship" that named best what church is for: "the New Testament concept of membership of the gathering or church of God's people in God's presence in heaven is a way of saying that we have fellowship through the gospel with God and Christ, and with one another.[17]

As participants in the heavenly gathering around God's throne formed by Christ, Christian believers already have a spiritual relationship with one another prior to any meeting together in an earthly sense. Their fellowship transcends any boundaries established by earthly denominations. This heavenly fellowship is a meeting that finds expression in assemblies of Christians as they gather. In fact, without meeting there is no fellowship. Fellowship in the present life "requires propinquity with a word and a response."[18] In the earthly sense, physical presence is required to express this fellowship which is the essence of church. Because of our humanness, these local, intermittent gatherings form patterns, which become in many instances the denominations that ought to service the local church. Knox differed somewhat from Robinson in that he saw that the church's relationship with God gives it a purpose: "because the relationship is God facing, it is fellowship with

15. Robinson, *Donald Robinson*, 1:242.
16. Robinson did insist that the gathered church should pray and seek to hear the Spirit's calling of individual evangelists as the word is ministered in the congregation. So the meeting is not quite as uninterested in evangelism as some of his other comments might suggest. See Robinson "The Doctrine of the Church," 162.
17. Knox, *D. Broughton Knox*, 2:21.
18. Ibid., 2:31.

God in his work with the world. God faces the world in saving love, and in him we face the world in saving love (i.e., in evangelism and works of charity and moral witness to society)."[19]

Evaluating Knox and Robinson

The insights of Knox and Robinson bring a remarkable clarity to matters of church polity. They assert the real, spiritual communion of all believers in Christ and at the same time emphasize the fellowship of the local congregation as the earthly manifestation of church. The denomination, or the communion, no matter how grand its claims or exalted its history, is a contingent affair—often given its shape by quirks of history and politics. It is a "service-structure" designed to support local congregations and ought to be treated as such and not more. Its relationships can have the nature of "fellowship" but they often prevent and even pervert it. This is not just in theory, either: local congregations in various parts of the Anglican Communion have been severely disciplined by diocesan officials with the loss of their property.

The looseness with which contemporary Protestant theologians continue to use the word "church" is checked by the Robinson-Knox insight. Particularly in the work of highly influential theologians such as Stanley Hauerwas from Duke University, "church" is used in a general sense and given enormous importance. And yet, it is hard to see how what Hauerwas is talking about actually accords with any scriptural description of church. In the face of the decline of the mainline denominations in the US, there is a hankering after a stronger view of church that might provide a community of practices to ground theological thinking. A number of well-publicized conversions to Roman Catholicism show how strongly this emphasis on the traditions and practices of "the church" has taken hold—and yet at the same time how difficult it is on the Protestant side to ground it in any actual ecclesial reality.[20] The emphasis on the local church congregation offers this grounding.

But the Knox-Robinson view of the church has its conceptual limitations. The fundamental polemical insight that exposed the pomposity

---

19. Robinson, "The Biblical Concept of Fellowship," 79–80.

20. The list includes theologians such as R. R. Reno, Douglas Farrow, Reinhard Hütter, and Bruce D. Marshall. See http://www.religion-online.org/showarticle.asp?title=3436.

of the denominational structures can remain. Yet any further thinking about "the church" must certainly seek to adjust the Knox-Robinson model where it is weakest. First: Robinson claimed that all references to *ekklesia* in the New Testament referred to actual gatherings of believers, whether the universal gathering in heaven or the local one on earth. There are however several references in the New Testament to "the church of God" that, on the best reading, do indeed seem to indicate a general, earthly church. In 1 Corinthians 15:9 and Galatians 1:13, Paul speaks of his former life when he persecuted the "church of God."[21] Quite obviously this cannot mean merely a single local church as it was in the act of gathering. In Acts 3:8 Saul as he then was is described going from house to house in order to drag off the believers to prison. In this act, he "began to destroy the church." The plurality of houses mentioned shows that it cannot have been a single church in its actual moment of gathering that is meant. This "church" was not "churching" yet was still an entity known as "church." Other instances seem to show the *ekklesia* terminology congealing into a collective term for the believers, whether in multiple locations with, one assumes, a multiplicity of church meetings in operation, or in the state of not meeting. In most modern translations (TNIV, NRSV, ESV) of Acts 9:31 we read: "Then *the church* throughout Judea, Galilee and Samaria enjoyed a time of peace and was strengthened." Textual critics examining the original manuscripts have decided that singular noun *ekklesia* is to be preferred to the plural *ekklesiai*, "churches," which is found in the 1611 Authorized Version. If the more modern reading of the text is taken as established, there is then a clear reference to a non-meeting, general "church."

We ought to grant that the emphasis of the NT is on the local gathering as *ekklesia*, but it is not as exclusive as Robinson made it seem. Whatever the case, the second query worth putting to the Knox-Robinson view is whether the method they employed is sufficiently *theological*. It is certainly a linguistic analysis of the usage of a particular word in the New Testament texts. Is this sufficient to provide for a proper *theological* description of the concept of "church"? Systematic theology has the task of inferring from the text what is appropriate and accurate

---

21. The reply has been given to these reading that either a) these singular references to "the church" in the context of Paul's testimony to his Damascus road encounter with Christ refer to the church in its gathered heavenly session around the throne of Christ or b) they are a "distributive singular." In both cases special pleading seems to be in evidence.

to say about revealed concepts in the light of the whole of the divine revelation. As a matter of convenience and habit it makes use of scriptural terminology to speak of the subjects it has to deal with. Thus, under the heading of "the doctrine of the church" or "ecclesiology" is placed a good deal more than a description of the usage of the word *ekklesia* in the NT. What Scripture says about the concept of "church" is not merely confined to the way it uses the particularly word "church." That *ekklesia* usually describes actual gatherings of people in the New Testament is not in fact grounds to limit the theological concept to actual particular gatherings. We could validly describe the denomination as "churchly" without conceding the priority of the local church as "church."

Third, the relationship between the earthly and the heavenly church has been insufficiently described, and the passages speaking of the heavenly gathering of the church made to do too much work. The notion of a "present heavenly gathering" is not as directly depicted as one would have assumed, given the ecclesiology that has been built on it. In both Ephesians and in Hebrews, the language of heavenly gathering needs to be understood as mediated through and in Christ. The list of images in Heb 12:22–3 is a way of describing the security and confidence that the believers have because of the sacrifice of Christ. The perfect tense "you have come" does not contradict the impression that what is being described is an eschatological reality, not a present one, as O'Brien agrees.[22] Likewise, in Ephesians 2:6–7, the heavenly gathering is the counterpart of the "in Christ" election of the believers from before the foundation of the world described in Ephesians 1. The believers do not have a dual nature, one secured in heaven and one more exposed ("manifested') on earth. On the contrary: they are represented in heaven by the mediator, Jesus Christ. *In him*, they are there—in a very specific and carefully conditioned sense. And the emphasis is on the eschatological disclosure which the believer awaits: in Eph 2:6–7, God has raised the believers with Christ so that he might show his grace in the coming ages.

We can see this anticipatory note in a couple of passages with more individual concerns in mind. The citizenship of the believer in heaven (Phil 3:20–21) so expects a savior from there. The life of the believer is hid with Christ in God so that when he appears "you will appear with him" (Col 3:1–4). In each of these depictions, the present

22. O'Brien, "The Church as a Heavenly and Eschatological Entity," 95.

heavenly reality is a Christological reality and is different from the coming reality at the last things. Just so, the local church is not then a "manifestation" of a gathering in heaven. It is a corollary of an identity secured and established *in Christ*. It is founded on the shared basis of Christ's representation of us to the Father—from which comes our holiness, forgiveness, and freedom. It is a reconciliation with God that enables and empowers and establishes a community of reconciliation on earth that foreshadows the coming transformation of all things. It is better described, as the Croatian evangelical theologian Miroslav Volf does, as an *anticipation* of the final heavenly gathering.[23] Modifying the notion of the heavenly gathering in this way modifies the structure of the proposed ecclesiology. Knox was quite insistent that the heavenly assembly had to be "a present, not merely future reality."[24] Yet it seems that this modification has to be embraced if exegetical and theological correctness amounts to anything in this discussion.

Fourth, the Knox-Robinson reading of church could be enriched by greater attention to the work of the Holy Spirit. In the Bible and in the creeds, the nexus between the Holy Spirit and the church is very strongly established. The church is united to Jesus Christ and represented by him in the heavenly throne room—but this is made possible by the mediation of the Holy Spirit. The church is the "temple of the Holy Spirit" (2 Cor 3:14). The unity of the church is the unity of the Spirit (Eph 4). The church is a creature of the Word, certainly, but it is also a creature of the Spirit who draws people to the Word. No one can say "Jesus is Lord" except by the Holy Spirit (1 Cor 12).

These conceptual weaknesses lead to a number of distortions in practice. Among them is the tendency to treat denominational structures somewhat pragmatically. If denominations are not "church," then leaving them is not strictly speaking schismatic. You are not dissolving the unity of the church by splitting a denomination if the denomination is not a church. Splitting a congregation is another matter altogether—though if we take the notion of intermittent meeting seriously, church-splitting would (bizarrely) have to take place at an actual gathering. The denomination is merely a property-holding company. However, having

---

23. Volf, *After Our Likeness*, 272. This is also Martin Foord's suggestion: "the local church anticipates the heavenly eschatological gathering into Christ's presence of all God's people" ("Recent Directions in Anglican Ecclesiology," 330).

24. Knox, *D. Broughton Knox*, 2:45.

rightly exposed the way in which denominations have colonized the notion of "church," it is a mistake to assume that there is nothing churchly about denominations. There is scriptural and theological warrant for recognizing a notion of the general church, as I have intimated, and denominations can fairly expect to be treated as a type of general, earthly church. The polemical overcorrection needs itself to be corrected. In a very real sense, this is one of the most important challenges facing Sydney Anglicans at the present time. Granted everything that has been said about the national "church," what does membership in that church look like? What responsibilities does it demand?

Knox once wrote: "The local gathering is the complete church of Christ, even if it only consists of two persons gathered in Christ's name, for he is there with them."[25] In a sense this is right. But it would be misleading to assert this without also asserting the way in which each earthly instance of the church is incomplete and imperfect. The church now is not what it will be. In anticipating (or even "manifesting") an eschatological church, the local gathering of believers does not establish a beachhead of perfection and ecclesial wholeness. It remains on a path towards the gathering that it will one day become by the transforming power of the Holy Spirit. If the church is *now* gathered in heaven by faith, in the sense that Knox and Robinson describe it, then it is possible to conceive of it as already perfected. The notion of "anticipation" prevents that possibly over-realized ecclesiology and its attendant dangers. Furthermore, there is the potential for the congregation to fail to recognize its need for fellowship with other congregations, though Knox himself warned against this years ago: "Christian fellowship is naturally not restricted within the local congregation; the congregation is the expression of the fellowship which is the church of Christ. This latter will overleap the limits of geography to create fellowship between congregations.[26]

What does this "fellowship" look like in the Anglican Church of Australia?

---

25. Ibid., 25.
26. Ibid., 27.

Current Ecclesiological Challenges

The Knox-Robinson doctrine of the church has encouraged a freedom of thought as regards the usual denominational structures in the name of mission and edification. It gave permission for a *laissez-faire* approach in the context of tightly controlled denominational economy. It is often forgotten by those who oppose the innovative and entrepreneurial spirit of contemporary evangelicalism that, even in the nineteenth century, the parishes and dioceses of the Church of England was crisscrossed by trusts, chapels, abbeys, colleges, and schools. The bureaucratic tightening and centralization of that church under the hegemony of the bishop is comparatively recent.

This entrepreneurial flexibility can breed a pragmatism that is forgetful of its theological roots. Sydney Anglicans have invested much of their hopes and expended much of their energy for missionary expansion in the strategy of church planting. The hope—the prayer—is that the rigidity of the old parish system will be broken open by an injection of new church communities led by vigorous young pastors. This strategy, once frowned upon by other Anglicans, has now been warmly commended by the General Synod of the Anglican Church of Australia at its 2010 meeting under the heading of "Fresh Expressions."

But the problem of the identity of Sydney's Anglicans *as Anglicans* still remains. Can such a flexible approach to ecclesiology coupled with an emphasis on the local congregation be accommodated under a recognizably Anglican way of doing things—especially under the constitution of the Anglican Church of Australia? And furthermore: with tensions in the worldwide Anglican Communion strained to breaking point, is there any point in identifying as Anglican any longer? It is to this matter that I turn in the next chapter.

seven

Are Sydney Anglicans Actually Anglicans?

Not Real Anglicans?

Are Sydney Anglicans actually Anglicans? If an Anglican from another part of Australia, or from the United Kingdom, walked into an ordinary Sydney Anglican parish on a Sunday morning would they recognize what they saw as being Anglican? The building may have a shape that echoes the distinctive shape of countless English parish churches. You are, however, unlikely to find a robed or collared clergyman leading the service—unless you come perhaps to the early morning service. While the structure and outline of the prayer book service will be in evidence, it will be used flexibly. The music will most likely be modern in style and the words projected on a large screen. The pipe organ and the pulpit will not be used. The prayers may well be *ex tempore*.

For some, there is no way in which what I have just described could be called "Anglican," because their notion of Anglicanism relates to a particular liturgical style. Without this particular style, in their mind, there is no Anglican identity. The assumption of course is that the particular style of liturgy that they have in mind is normative for Anglican worship throughout history and in every place—and that Anglicanism itself permits little or no variation in that form. This point of view reflects the almost complete supremacy in most Western countries of the liberal Catholic paradigm of Anglicanism, with its emphasis on liturgy over doctrine.

Are Sydney Anglicans Actually Anglicans?

Evangelical Anglicans, however, have a commitment to Anglicanism as a *theological* entity. That is, they recognize that even if Anglicanism is not as strictly confessional as some other churches, it still has doctrinal parameters. There is, for Anglicans, a core of orthodoxy around which all manner of stylistic variations are permitted and even welcomed. The needs of mission and local custom make liturgical flexibility desirable—a practicality that the Anglican formularies of the sixteenth century themselves recognize. What is consistent as far as evangelical Anglicans are concerned—or ought to be consistent—is a common faith. They are Anglicans not merely by convenience but by conviction.

My purpose in this chapter is twofold. On the one hand, it is to show that Sydney Anglicans are the inheritors of an Anglicanism that has a long and deeply established heritage in the Church of England and that they share in an expression of Anglicanism that is, in global terms, widespread. Far from being an Anglican aberration caused by a quirk of history or a narrow ultra-Protestant sect, they can trace their way of being Anglican in continuous line back to the Reformation and even somewhat before. Those who question the Anglican-ness of Sydney Anglicans do so tendentiously. On the other hand, it is my purpose to urge Sydney's evangelical Anglicans not to cave in to the critics. The constant barrage of criticism on this front ought not to lead Sydney Anglicans to despise or neglect their own Anglican roots. As I will show with a brief sketch here, the classic Anglican description of the supreme authority of Scripture resonates enormously with the evangelicalism that is found in most parishes in Sydney. Their Anglican past provides deep wells from which fresh water may be drawn.

Protestant Anglicanism

What is an "Anglican"? In one sense the term itself is anachronistic. The Church of England is primarily an institution, the national church of a particular country. It was only with the growth of the British Empire that the question of "Anglicanism" arose—especially when there was now a political separation between England and the United States of America. The Episcopal Church of the US was not governed by the King of England from 1776—so in what sense could it, and other former Church of England churches, understand their continuity with the church that had given them birth? It was an identity question that was felt with a particular pressure in the nineteenth century and which has decisive significance for the way we consider the question of "Anglicanism" today.

Those of more Catholic disposition have emphasized the continuity of the English church today with the church of the pre-Reformation period. Even when it was in communion with the Church of Rome, the English church (the *ecclesia Anglicana*) had its own remarkable and somewhat independent identity. The tension between the papacy and the English monarchy—which came to a head in the Reformation—had many precedents, including the murder of the archbishop of Canterbury, Thomas Beckett, in 1170 by King Henry II's henchmen. However, any assertion of a continuity of heritage between the pre-Reformation church and what came later has to reckon with the complexity and diversity of that history. For example, in the seventh century AD both Celtic and Roman styles of Christianity competed for supremacy in the English Church. Which is to be held as more authentically "Anglican"? Or is it a synthesis between them? Where in the story does the radicalism of the Oxford scholar John Wyclif (1330–1378) and the movement of his followers, the Lollards, fit in? That is to say: describing a continuous line from the pre-Reformation period to the present has more challenges than the standard Anglo-Catholic description allows. The demand for reform and the appeal to the authority of Scripture is part of the picture that ought not to be obscured.[1]

Since the 1980s, revisionist historians such as Christopher Haigh and Eamon Duffy have tried to describe the English Reformation as a top-down and chiefly political movement that had little traction among the English people themselves. There is no doubt that the English Reformation was achieved through the workings of statecraft as much as through the conversion of souls. Henry VIII's "great matter"—the problem of his barren marriage to Catherine of Aragon—was the catalyst not only for an institutional break with the Church of Rome and with the papacy, but for a change in the theological outlook of the English church. While Haigh and Duffy try to paint this as almost entirely engineered by a coterie of theologians like Archbishop Thomas Cranmer (1489–1556), there is no question but that the faith of Reformation

---

1. Turnbull, *Anglican and Evangelical?*, 10.

Europe had made some inroads among the English people in the 1520s, however clandestine.[2]

Thomas Cranmer is not a figure for Anglicans in the same way Martin Luther is for Lutherans. Nonetheless, Cranmer's Reformation bequeathed to the English church a particular theological outlook that cannot be eclipsed in any description of Anglican identity. Though some have tried, Oxford historian Richard Turnbull notes "It is difficult to deny the formative role of the Reformation on the polity, theology and ministry of the Church of England."[3] It is certainly appropriate to use terms like "Protestant" and "Reformed" when speaking about Anglicanism.

Cranmer set down three large foundation stones upon which henceforth the English church was built: the *Thirty-Nine Articles of Religion*, the *Book of Common Prayer*, and the *Ordinal*. These have not come down to us unaltered from his pen. They were subject to a degree of refinement and alteration. Even so, the attempt to minimize the importance of these formularies in some parts of the Anglican Communion in recent years only reveals an embarrassment with the unabashed Protestantism of these documents. That is: they express a "protest" against the Roman Catholic Church and a theology that was itself moving away from Lutheranism and is mainly learned from the Reformed churches in Germany and Switzerland. This theology took its lead from Luther in upholding that justification was by grace alone through faith but had begun to develop an emphasis on the sovereignty of God and on the doctrine of predestination. It was also moving away from Luther's description of the "real presence" of Christ in the elements of bread and wine at the Eucharist and towards a more vague sense that he was present to the believer at the event "by faith." South African Anglican scholar Nicholas H. Taylor notes that these three documents "became a definitive expression of Anglican doctrine and discipline."[4] While it would be historically naïve to think of the career of Cranmer as the reset point for Anglican identity—as if nothing has happened since then, or as if he is an Anglican Muhammad—it is certainly the case that no description of Anglican identity can bypass or minimize his contribution to the theological distinctiveness of Anglicanism.

2. MacCulloch, *Reformation*, 204.
3. Turnbull, *Anglican and Evangelical?*, 14.
4. Taylor, *Lay Presidency at the Eucharist*, 13.

"Unabashed Protestantism": is that an overstatement? That the liturgy was now to be in the vernacular was in itself recognition of a different—Protestant—understanding of the very nature of Christian faith itself. The words of the prayer book were not meant to be experienced by the people as a mystery evading their understanding. The service of Holy Communion was, in successive editions of the prayer book, moving in a more Protestant or "Reformed" direction. Recent work by renowned Oxford historian Diarmaid MacCulloch (1951–) shows that Cranmer's eucharistic theology was becoming even less like Luther's understanding of the "real presence" and shifting towards a Reformed understanding.[5] The document that became *The Thirty-Nine Articles of Religion* is unmistakably Reformed in character. It is true that the articles do allow for a deal of flexibility, and do not pronounce on some controversial matters. Yet that should not be mistaken for some policy of reticence or the endorsement of infinite variety. The embarrassment of liberal and Catholic Anglicans at the *Articles* is a fairly strong indication that the plain reading of them sees them as an expression of a Reformed theological outlook.

The *Articles* assert the primacy of the authority of Scripture for Anglican faith and practice. That is not to say that Scripture is the *only* authority, but it is held to be the supreme authority, even over the great creeds of the church (article 8). Article 6 reads: "Holy Scripture containeth all things necessary to salvation: so that whatsoever is not read therein, nor may be proved thereby, is not to be required of any man, that it should be believed as an article of the Faith, or be thought requisite or necessary to salvation." According to the articles, Scripture is to act as the measure of what Anglicans believe.

For two great Elizabethan Anglicans, Scripture was likewise of paramount importance. First, in his 1562 work *Apology of the Church in England,* Bishop John Jewel (1522–1571) of Salisbury made an ardent defense of the Reformation settlement in England, setting it over against the abuses of the Church of Rome. He depicted the Church of England as episcopal, but thoroughly Reformed in doctrine. The Church of England in its stance against Rome needed to be convincingly apostolic. It could do so by appeal to Scripture; but also by appeal to the Church Fathers and to the councils. This was not to invest them with an authority independent of Scripture, but to show that, even on

---

5. MacCulloch, *Thomas Cranmer*, 405.

their preferred ground, the Roman Church was not the true heir of the apostolic teaching.

The second of these men was Richard Hooker (1554–1600), often held up as the doyen of Anglican divines—"judicious," rational, careful, and moderate in tone. His significance to subsequent debates about Anglican identity is not reflected by the impact he made on the Church of England in his own day, which was quite minimal.[6] He was an opponent of the Puritan extremists in the Church of England who were moving against the episcopate and against all customs not explicitly sanctioned in Scripture. For a long time, the standard reading of Hooker was that he had endorsed "the three-legged stool" of Scripture, reason, and tradition as equal, mutually-informing authorities in Anglican thinking. It is a myth that still persists. Careful reading of Hooker's *Ecclesiastical Polity* tells another story. He writes, "What Scripture doth plainly deliver, to that first place both of credit and obedience is due; the next whereunto is whatsoever any man can necessarily conclude by force of reason; after these the voice of the Church succeedeth. That which the Church by her ecclesiastical authority shall probably think and define to be true or good, must in congruity of reason over-rule all other inferior judgments whatsoever."[7]

Scripture, reason, and tradition do not have equal weight for Hooker. Quite clearly, Scripture has precedence, then reason, and third, church tradition. Though the Puritans were mistaken when they opposed tradition where Scripture was silent, they were correct in placing Scripture ahead of all other authorities. Hooker can be described as endorsing the "normative" view of Scripture with regard to church order and ceremonies, as opposed to the "regulative" view championed by his Puritan opponents such as William Perkins (1558–1602) and Thomas Cartwright (1535–1603).[8] He conceded that the threefold order of ministry—bishop, priest, and deacon—cannot be directly established from Scripture, but that the historic episcopate is nevertheless a good way to frame the polity of the English church.[9]

---

6. MacCulloch, *Reformation*, 506.

7. Hooker, *The Folger Library Edition*, 5:8:2.

8. The "normative" principle holds that Christian worship can include those things not prohibited in Scripture. The "regulative" principle holds that worship ought only to include those activities explicitly licensed in Scripture.

9. A recent editor notes that Hooker was not "a proto-Tractarian, promoting an

Sydney Anglicanism

The Elizabethan Settlement is sometimes described by contemporary Anglicans as a *via media* between Rome and Geneva. To read the writings of some of the leading supporters of Elizabeth's religious policy is not to sense a spirit of compromise with Rome, however. Like the queen they served, Hooker and Jewel were adamant in their Protestantism even if they differed in degrees of vehemence. What they were arguing about was which variety of Protestantism they would endorse and to what extent. It was more accurately described as a *via media* between Martin Luther's Wittenberg and John Calvin's Geneva.

What these examples prove is quite modest, but it is sufficient. They demonstrate that those who hold that it is thoroughly and authentically Anglican to view Scripture as the supreme authority have a more than reasonable case grounded in the major documents of Anglican history and in the thought of its major theologians. Furthermore, on soteriology (the theory of how one is saved) and the sacraments, it is quite clearly possible to discern a succession of authoritative figures and documents that assert a Reformed view, however distasteful this might be to some contemporary Anglicans. There are other readings of Anglican history, most notably the reading perpetuated by the Oxford Movement in the nineteenth century, that emphasized the "Caroline divines" of the early seventeenth century and their appeal to the church fathers. Yet even the sketch of Anglicanism I have provided here shows that the Oxford Movement's reading of Anglican history could only ever be a selective and polemical one. A Christian faith which places it emphasis on the supreme authority of Scripture for doctrine and practice and which upholds a Reformed view of salvation and the sacraments can with confidence assert its continuous place within the Anglican story. A view of Anglicanism which places Scripture as supreme authority and which has a Reformed soteriology and which has a flexible attitude to secondary matters, such as liturgical practice, certainly has a good case to be considered as authentically Anglican.

However, this plurality and flexibility is not infinite. While Scripture is authoritative in all the Anglican formularies, there are also certain conditions under which Scripture ought to be received. The great creeds are not merely summary statements of scriptural teaching. They are the way in which Scripture ought to be read for Anglicans. For

---

Anglican via media" but instead "a man of the Reformation in the Calvinist tradition" (Chapman, *Law and Revelation*, 21).

example, it is axiomatic that Anglicanism is a trinitarian form of Christianity. Positing the authority of Scripture does not allow for revision of that article of faith. While the assumption of the *Articles* is that the church submits to Scripture, and that the church may certainly err, even when it sits in council, there is no sense in which a reconfiguration of orthodoxy itself is envisaged. Likewise, it would be hard to imagine an Anglican church that did not accept and practice the two sacraments, or one that was non-episcopal.

The Puritans in the Church of England

Sydney Anglicans more often than not trace their heritage to the great Church of England figures of the sixteenth century—to Cranmer, to the martyred bishops Latimer and Ridley, and to the others who were leaders under Edward VI and martyred under his sister Mary. Marcus Loane (1911–2009), archbishop of Sydney from 1966–1981 and formerly principal of Moore College, authored a number of popular histories of this period after the manner of John Foxe's *Acts and Monuments of the English Church*.[10] The defiant stance of these figures on the basis of the Protestant and Reformed character of the Church of England was a marker of identity in 1950s and 60s Australia—a period in which sectarianism was much more prominent as a social issue than it is today, and a period in which the Anglo-Catholic movement within the Anglican Church of Australia was making a great deal of headway. As the national church came together, would Sydney Anglicans remain true to the faith for which the great Marian martyrs died? Certainly they would.

The somewhat romantic appeal to the martyrdoms of the Marian reign is a hint that a particular reading of the course of the English Reformation is in place: that the short reign of Edward VI was a Protestant high watermark for the Church of England, but that the program begun in that brief period (1547–1553) had remained unfinished. On this reading of the English Reformation, there is some sympathy for those who later chafed at the slow rate of change under Elizabeth's rule and who became known as "the Puritans." It is one of those words—like "fundamentalist"—that has become (indeed always was) a religious

10. For example, Loane, *Masters of the English Reformation*; Loane, *Oxford and the Evangelical Succession*; Loane, *Cambridge and the Evangelical Succession*.

term of abuse, with its image of humorless and stern moral nitpickers. This label has been frequently applied to Sydney Anglicans by their detractors not only to indicate their determination to further reform Anglicanism along Protestant lines but also to describe their alleged moral seriousness.[11]

Historically speaking, the label "Puritan" is a broad brush. There were Puritans over the long period of their prominence (from 1560s through to 1680s) who strongly disagreed with each other over what needed to change in the Church and which doctrines to emphasize. Ultimately it was the Puritans of Parliament who rose up against the forces of Charles I and had him executed in 1649, inaugurating the Protectorate of Oliver Cromwell (1653–1658). Puritans were at various times persecuted and even expelled by the Church authorities. Yet at the same time, the presence within the Church of England of those who might identify with the Puritan disposition has been ongoing. As Richard Turnbull has written "Throughout the history of the Church of England there has also been a persecution of Puritan divines and yet also a continuing presence within the Church of those of Puritan disposition."[12] This was so even after the "Great Ejection," when nearly two thousand Puritan clergy chose to leave their livings in protest against the 1662 Act of Uniformity. Interestingly, it was the issue of the royal supremacy which was most controversial. The restoration of the *Book of Common Prayer*, somewhat modified in line with Puritan sensibilities, was not nearly as problematic.

To identify with the Puritans, then, is not to repudiate Anglicanism. It is certainly to insist on the importance of right doctrine and on the propriety of ongoing reform of church practices in line with Scripture—and this is not to the taste of some other Anglicans. Some streams of Puritanism certainly found themselves outside the Church of England. Those Puritans who would advocate presbyterianism, for example, found themselves outside of the bounds of the Church of England following the Restoration. It would be hard to make the case for a non-episcopal version of Anglicanism today. On matters of church governance, discipline, and order, the "normative" rather than the "regulative" principle holds sway with Anglicanism. However, it was

---

11. See for example the title of Muriel Porter's book, *The New Puritans—The Rise of Fundamentalism in the Anglican Church*.

12. Turnbull, *Anglican and Evangelical?*, 32.

frequently matters to do with church-state relations that led to the rebellion and then departure of Puritan clergy from the established church. It is fascinating to note that this was the very goad against which the Oxford Movement kicked. John Keble's famous 1833 sermon "National Apostasy" was an attack on the collaboration of the Church of England with its government. For Anglicans not now living in England under royal supremacy, this issue is entirely irrelevant. What this means is that Puritans have had a long-standing place within the Church of England and within Anglicanism; and that on one of the major issues on which they took their stand (royal supremacy), they were not the only ones to do so. If Sydney Anglicans are Puritans, or at least claim to stand in their tradition, it does not follow that they are not also Anglicans.

Evangelicals and Anglicans

If Sydney Anglicans identify somewhat with the Puritans, especially of the Elizabethan era, it is also the case that they identify very strongly with the "evangelical" movement of the eighteenth century. The first chaplains of the colony were evangelicals and sponsored by the circle of Charles Simeon, one of the leading evangelicals of the Church of England. Like the Puritan movement, this was a movement that began within but subsequently exceeded the bounds of the Church of England. The established Church proved too limiting for many and also sought to persecute and expel the proponents of evangelicalism.[13] And yet, there is no doubt that evangelicalism has played and continues to play a major part in the history and ethos of Anglicanism. As Turnbull says, "Anglican evangelicalism is a manifestation of the Christian faith which gives fullness of expression to the core foundational beliefs of both Anglican and evangelical Christian traditions."[14]

Most commonly, the evangelical movement is thought to have begun in the eighteenth century with the conversion of John Wesley in 1738. Labeled "enthusiasts" by their opponents in the Church of England, the evangelicals were treated with a great deal of hostility and found difficulty in obtaining livings. This "enthusiasm," though it seemed crass to some of their co-religionists, was representative of

13. I have in mind especially John Wesley (1703–1791) and his followers, the "Methodists."

14. Turnbull, *Anglican and Evangelical?*, 123.

an extraordinary reawakening of ardent faith. It was a direct reaction against the dryness, formalism, and rationalism that characterized much of early eighteenth-century established Christianity.[15] A Christianity without a heart for God was clearly deficient. The evangelical movement lead to missionary zeal and social reform on a grand scale; evangelicals formed societies and cooperated trans-denominationally. They wrote hymns that are still sung today. Wesley and Whitfield become famous as open-air preachers. Like the Puritans, it is has to be said that the evangelicals oftentimes inhabited the fringes of the institutional Church. They seemed less interested in ecclesiastical preferment and more concerned with missionary work.

The term "evangelical" itself is contested territory, both as a historical description and as a identifier for contemporary Christians. My purpose here is not to become entangled in this debate, but simply to show with broad brush strokes that evangelicalism and Anglicanism overlap considerably. Anglicanism is a great denominational home for evangelicalism, but it is not the only one. Likewise, evangelicalism has made and continues to make a considerable contribution to Anglicanism. The British historian David Bebbington's (1949–) description of evangelicalism is the best known and most widely used and will be sufficient to frame our discussion here.[16] Bebbington speaks of "a quadrilateral of priorities"—namely: conversionism, activism, Biblicism, and crucicentricism.

Evangelicals are conversionist in that they proclaim the necessity of personal transformation in response to the gospel of grace. They preach to the heart, appealing for repentance from sin and turning to God in dependence. Their gospel is highly individualist in this sense—it is not sufficient for true Christian faith merely to be in possession of membership in a church grouping. Evangelicals are also, as Bebbington speaks of them, activist. They expected the evangelical conversion to result in a transformation of life. This meant that the believer was expected to be busy in the process of moral renewal and in seeking the conversion and moral renewal of others. The activism characteristic of evangelicals resulted in evangelistic mission but also in programs for social welfare on a large scale. Evangelicals such as William Wilberforce

---

15. Ibid., 54.
16. Bebbington, *Evangelicalism in Modern Britain*.

and the Earl of Shaftesbury become bywords for the activist streak within evangelicalism.

Evangelicals have always been people of the Bible. Like their Reformation forebears, they have taken Scripture as the supreme authority for Christian life and for doctrine. The centrality of preaching for evangelicals is evidence of what this means in practice. As well as being biblicist, the evangelical is also crucicentric—which means that central place is given to the atoning work of Christ on the cross. Christ is an exemplary figure and a moral teacher, but he is first and foremost the savior who died for sin.

In bringing Anglicanism and evangelicalism together, Anglican evangelicals have mostly but not exclusively subscribed to a form of moderate Calvinism. This description would apply to the faith of two of the greatest of evangelical Anglicans, Charles Simeon (1759–1836) and Bishop J. C. Ryle (1816–1900). They appealed for their identity within Anglicanism to the Protestant and Reformed nature of the Anglican settlements of the sixteenth and seventeenth century. However, they did not insist on the rigorous application of Reformed doctrine, especially over the extent of the atonement. Just as article 17 is quite a restrained account of predestination, so Anglican evangelicals have certainly asserted but not overemphasized this teaching. Most often cooperation in evangelism and fellowship with non-Calvinist evangelicals overrode concerns about absolute purity of doctrine. Even if the effects of the atonement were to be applied only to the elect, the preaching of the gospel was to be to all.

This ethos is perhaps where tension with the institutional framework of Anglicanism most often surfaces. More often than not, evangelicals have felt themselves excluded from the positions of power within the Anglican churches of the West. Their priority has always been the preaching of the gospel and not the maintenance of the institutional church. Their ecclesiology—and this is especially the case in Sydney, as we have seen—does not tend to recognize the bureaucratic side of the denomination as "church." If the institution inhibits the preaching of the gospel, then there is no question where compromise has to be made. For other Anglicans with a more hierarchical view this seems like schismatic behavior.

As the Oxford Movement grew in influence in the middle part of the nineteenth century, the evangelicals insisted on the Protestantism of the Church of England, often to the point of legal controversy. The most celebrated—or notorious, depending on your point of view—of these incidents was the "Gorham case" of 1846–1847. Evangelical clergyman Charles Gorham clashed with his Tractarian bishop Henry Phillpotts over the critical issue of infant baptism. Gorham, taking the evangelical position, asserted that baptism did not necessarily effect regeneration—it did not make you a saved Christian, in other words. After all, evangelicals believed in the necessity of repentance and conversion. Phillpotts pointed to the wording of the *Book of Common Prayer* that seems to refer to the child as regenerate and wanted to refuse him a post in his diocese as a man of unsound doctrine. The precedent set by the case could have made the position of every evangelical clergyman in England uncertain, to say the least. The case made its way as far as the non-ecclesiastical Judicial Committee of the Privy Council, which finally found for Gorham. What this meant was that the legal place of evangelicals within the Church of England was (somewhat ingloriously) secured. Their interpretation of the formularies was certainly permitted, if not entirely endorsed.

In Sydney there is an entire diocese in a major city that is run by evangelicals. This breaks with the usual experience of evangelicals as having almost no institutional leverage and in having to live within diocesan structures which are liberal Catholic in flavor. The evangelical behaviors which have irritated non-evangelical Anglicans historically are magnified in the case of Sydney. The unusual dominance of evangelicals in the diocesan structure of Sydney diocese means that Sydney does look strange to Anglicans who are accustomed to liberal Catholic hegemony—and ecclesiology—elsewhere. Liberal Catholics *expect* to be in charge of things. But they would be mistaken in calling evangelicalism "unAnglican," for the moderate Calvinist evangelical outlook of Sydney with its missionary activism and its biblicism and with its emphasis on the atoning blood of Jesus Christ as a sacrifice for sins is utterly consistent with the evangelical Anglican tradition that has had an unbroken presence in the Church of England for nearly three centuries. The English evangelical Anglican scholar Alister McGrath has written, "My concern is simply to insist that evangelicalism is, historically and theologically, a legitimate and respectable option within Anglicanism. At no point is evangelicalism inconsistent with any of the Thirty-Nine

Articles, the only document apart from Scripture, the creeds and the Prayer Book, regarded as authoritative for Anglicans."[17]

It has not only been my intention to show here that Sydney's evangelical Anglicans have a legitimate place within Anglicanism. History shows that the evangelicalism held so dear by Sydney's Anglicans arose from and was to a great extent nurtured by Anglicanism. Will this continue to be the case? It is to that question that we now turn.

To Stay or To Go?

While the Puritan and evangelical heritage of Sydney Anglicans gives them ample grounds to stake out within the Anglican tradition and to resist being marginalized, the reality to be admitted is that both of these groups have had at times testy relationships with the structural and institutional side of Anglicanism. Puritans were frustrated with the lack of further progress in doctrinal and liturgical reform and so many of them left the Church of England or were forced out. Evangelical Anglicans have always freely cooperated with evangelicals in other denominations, and have prioritized gospel work at the expense of institutional conformity. As Turnbull writes, "Historically, Anglican evangelicals have proved flexible over church order in the interests of the gospel."[18] But if Anglicanism has been flexible enough to accommodate evangelicals, it has also been flexible with progressive liberalism. Evangelicals have felt stymied in their mission by an institution which in turn seems only too ready to endorse the liberal agenda in faith and conduct. For evangelical Anglicans in every generation the question arises: "what is the tipping point as far as remaining an Anglican goes?"

It was certainly an issue for evangelicals in the latter part of the nineteenth century. Could they continue to preach the gospel unhindered in the Church of England when ritualism and liberalism were advancing? At a gathering of evangelical clergy from the Eastern Counties on the June 11, 1879, Bishop J. C. Ryle of Liverpool delivered this stirring call to remain:

> No doubt you live in days when our time-honored church is in a very perilous, distressing and critical position. Her rowers have

---

17. France and McGrath, *Evangelical Anglicans*, 13.
18. Turnbull, *Anglican and Evangelical?*, 120.

brought her into troubled water. Her very existence is endangered by papists, infidels, and liberationists without. Her lifeblood is drained away by the behavior of traitors, false friends and timid officers within. Nevertheless, so long as the Church of England sticks firmly to the Bible, the Articles, and the principles of the Protestant Reformation, so long I advise you strongly to stick to the church. When the Articles are thrown overboard, and the old flag is hauled down, then, and not till then, it will be time for you and me to launch the boats and quit the wreck. At present, let us stick to the old ship . . . Why should we leave her now, like cowards, because she is in difficulties, and the truth cannot be maintained within her pale without trouble? To whom can we go? Where shall we find better prayers? In what communion shall we find so much good being done, in spite of the existence of much evil? No doubt there is much to sadden us; but there is not a single visible church on earth at this day doing better. There is not a single communion where there are no clouds, and all is serene.[19]

The evangelical Anglican concedes that he or she is not a member of a pure church, or a purely Reformed church. But it is, as Ryle says, a theological mistake to expect purity and unity in any visible church.

A similar crisis point came in October 1966 when the free church preacher Dr. Martyn Lloyd-Jones (1899–1981), speaking at the National Assembly of Evangelicals, called upon evangelical clergy in denominations that were not exclusively evangelical to leave and to join with him in forming an evangelical denomination in which doctrinal purity could be assured. It seemed at the time like a reasonable appeal to evangelicals in the Church of England, who were increasingly marginalized and on the defensive and who had watched openly radical scholars such as J. A. T. Robinson (1919–1983) rewarded for their unorthodoxy by elevation to the episcopate. At this point, the acknowledged leader of the Anglican evangelicals, John Stott, intervened. This led to the wholesale recommitment of evangelicals to working within the Church of England in 1967 at the first National Evangelical Anglican Congress at Keele.[20] A similar conference was held in Australia but with no lasting impact.

---

19. Ryle, *Holiness*, 307.

20. For a full account of the Lloyd-Jones/Stott debate and the lasting impact of Stott on global evangelicalism, see Chapman, *Godly Ambition*.

Encouraged by the lead of John Stott, evangelicals in the Anglican Communion have largely held their ground. In the last forty years, the Anglican denominational structures have been in many cases quite congenial to the missional aspirations of evangelicals. Where other types of Anglican churches have waned, evangelical churches have certainly not. In that time the increase of evangelical numbers in the churches of the West has opened up new divisions, it must be granted. Tensions over the emphasis on charismatic gifts and the ministry of women continue to simmer. The consecration of woman as bishops, which is supported by many evangelicals, may prove to be a step too far for some more conservative evangelicals in the Church of England.

For Sydney's Anglican evangelicals then there is every good reason to remain committed to the Anglican Church. Sydney Anglicans have felt concern at developments in the national and global Anglican Communion and have frequently wondered aloud whether they could continue in fellowship with these bodies or what form that fellowship might take. They ought to remember that, as well as being an age of terrible division and confusion, the last forty years have been an era of remarkable innovation and experimentation in the name of mission, and there is much for which to give thanks. Sydney Anglicans have, quite suddenly, found themselves with opportunities to support gospel work in some of the most difficult parts of the world for Christian witness—in Myanmar, in Egypt, and in the Sudan, for example. Often the Anglicans in these places do not identify as "evangelical," but they are happy for the help of fellow orthodox Christians. The GAFCON[21] movement, in which Sydney Anglicans have played a central role, has provided the opportunity for a renewal of the notion of a global *confessing* Anglicanism.

Sydney Anglicans should not imagine that the giving is all in one direction in these encounters. If it is increasingly the case that Sydney Anglicans are being called on to contribute to national and international Anglicanism, it is also the case that they are being given an opportunity to learn and grow. Though it hasn't been commonly observed, being Anglican has contributed to the intellectual robustness and vigor of Sydney's *evangelicalism*. This is the promise of the future, too; the ties that are being strengthened with African and Asian and South American Anglicans is to the great benefit of Sydney Anglicans. They stand to

21. The acronym is formed from the title Global Anglican Future Conference.

profit considerably from the Christlike example and witness of faithful Christians in other parts of the world.

Yet if Sydney Anglicans want to stay within the fellowship of Anglican churches they need to do so in good faith. They ought to be Anglicans, as evangelical Anglicans have traditionally been, not only of convenience but of conviction. They cannot point the finger at those who transgress in the areas of faith and conduct if they themselves are in the process of eroding the Anglican edifice. For example, the supreme authority of Scripture in Anglicanism is given a particular mode of reception—by dint of the two great creeds, the sacraments and the role of the episcopate. Anglicanism is not a tradition in which every interpretation of Scripture is held to be equally valid—even if there is considerable room for disagreement. This is in contrast to churches that subscribe to the Westminster Confession of Faith, for example, which is far more detailed. It may be that, in all good conscience, some evangelical Christians need to admit that the Anglican expression of Christianity is not for them. They would not be the first.

Anglicanism doesn't require much, but it does require some things. Just as it is not possible to remain Anglican and to deny the resurrection or the Trinity with any integrity, it is not possible to remain Anglican with any authenticity and honesty and to have a greatly reduced role for the Lord's Supper and baptism. These examples are not equally serious, of course. But still: a church that substituted the practice of the Lord's Supper for a fellowship tea would not be an Anglican church and should have the honesty to say so. It may still be a *Christian* church, but it could not continue as an *Anglican* church. This is a challenge to Sydney Anglicans, since they have urged for liturgical change to do with the sacraments in particular.

Article 34 of the *Thirty-Nine Articles* (*Of the Traditions of the Church*) reads thus: "It is not necessary that traditions and ceremonies be in all places one or utterly alike; for at all times they have been diverse, and may be changed according to the diversity of countries, times, and men's manners, so that nothing be ordained against God's word."

There is here envisaged a liturgical flexibility. Modifications can and should be made for the customs of the place. Christians do not meet according to a rigidly fixed pattern or aping the historical dress and customs of a time gone by. But the principle is normative, not regulative;

that is, freedom is allowed insofar as it is constrained by God's word, rather than it being dictated lock stock and barrel by it. Indeed, the last sentence of the article is this: "Every particular or national Church hath authority to ordain, change, and abolish ceremonies or rites of the Church ordained only by man's authority, so that all things be done to edifying." So: have confirmation by a bishop, or don't have confirmation (for example).

But the middle section of the article reads: "Whosoever through his private judgment willingly and purposely doth openly break the traditions and ceremonies of the Church which be not repugnant to the word of God, and be ordained and approved by common authority, ought to be rebuked openly that others may fear to do the like, as he that offendeth against common order of the Church, and hurteth the authority of the magistrate, and woundeth the conscience of the weak brethren."

That is: even though there is a freedom for individual "particular" or "national" churches to change the style (for want of a better word) of their services—and indeed they ought to do so as the need arises—it is also most definitely *not* a matter of private judgment. It is not a matter of the local clergy varying the practices without authorization and/or consultation. Why is that? Because of the weak consciences of the faithful and because the authority set up to govern the Church is undermined by the practice.

Notice that, while on the one hand there is not a whiff that the agreed liturgical practice is soteriologically significant, or that it can't be varied or even radically changed, this is not in tension with the importance of maintaining church order. In a lot of discussions about church practices, this subtlety is not expressed. Church order is the way in which each church or fellowship of churches puts into practice the kind of teaching we receive from Paul in 1 Corinthians 8–14. It does not substitute for that teaching: it expresses it, for "God is not a God of chaos but of peace." The Church's observance of ordered corporate worship is a reflection of the character of God himself. Ordered doesn't mean "formal" or not relaxed or inauthentic. It just means that things are done in the meeting are consistent with the purpose of mutual edification.

That the sacraments are practiced is certainly not optional as far as the *Articles* are concerned because these were rites not instituted by man's authority, but by the Lord (see articles 25–31). It is hard to see how anyone could possibly argue that the sacraments themselves are optional, or merely "helpful," and remain Anglican in any meaningful sense. But *how* the sacraments might be practiced may indeed be varied on the condition that this is not a matter of private judgment because of the kind of troubling disorder that reflects badly on the God whose name we seek to honor. I hasten to add that the *Articles* certainly don't make this a free-for-all. They do not endorse those practices which communicate an essentially Roman Catholic view of the Supper: elevating the host, carrying it about, and so on. All of these concerns are flagrantly ignored in much Anglican practice, it ought to be said. The history of the Oxford Movement involved, bizarrely, a good deal of disregard for church order in the name of church order.

We have seen that the Sydney diocese regards itself as a "particular" church. It has characteristically read the Constitution of the Anglican Church of Australia as upholding the independent authority of each diocese and only then the authority of the national Church.[22] In that sense, it is entirely in keeping with this article—and the Constitution—for it to make its own decisions about how it will express its Anglican identity in the context of prayerful debate and given due consultation. It rightly resists greater centralization, especially when it is legal and coercive.

But identifying as Anglican, on any reading, involves you in a global and historical fellowship with which to be in conversation. As those who count themselves heirs of the Protestants, the Puritans, and the evangelicals, Sydney Anglicans share in a legitimate and in fact honored heritage within the Anglican Church. They ought to relish this rich legacy and remain within it, both to strengthen it and be strengthened by it.

---

22. Sydney is not alone in valuing its independent identity as a diocese. Bruce Kaye writes of the "historical pattern of diocesan independence in Australia as compared with a more national profile in England" (Kaye, *A Church Without Walls*, 112).

eight

The Church and the World

The Scripture in Schools Debate

In 2010, the New South Wales state government led by its then premier Kristina Keneally went ahead with a long-touted plan to trial classes in ethics as an alternative to Special Religious Education (SRE), or "Scripture," in the state's public schools.

Since the nineteenth century, when government schools were first built and education was made compulsory for children in NSW, provision for regular teaching of religious education by the churches (and subsequently other religious groups) was made in the timetable as part of the Public Schools Act itself.[1] This deal was made in exchange for the Church giving up many of its own schools. For more than a century, then, local clergy and their helpers have been allowed a weekly place in the timetable of otherwise nonsectarian schools. The classes were not compulsory—those children whose parents did not want them to go to Scripture could opt out of the classes. Under the terms of the agreement, no alternative program was to be run that might detract from SRE, or make the SRE children feel that they were missing out in some way. A principal could not, for example, offer an extension math class at that time.

---

1. The Public Schools Acts (1866) was followed by the Public Instruction Act (1880). The 1990 Education Act specifically prohibits non-scripture students being taught while others receive religious instruction.

For much of the 140 years since the inception of this practice, only a handful of students may have opted out of Scripture classes.[2] Since the 1970s, with growing secularization and a more aggressive and even stridently anti-Christian sentiment making itself felt in Australian culture, the numbers of parents whose children were not taking Scripture classes rose. The thought that their children were sitting idle for half an hour of the school week while some other children had classes in religious education seemed incomprehensible to them. An approach was made to the NSW government by the NSW Parents & Citizens groups to provide ethics classes as an alternative to SRE, and the St. James Ethics Institute was commissioned to provide a curriculum for these classes.

The classes went to trial in 2010. It was supposed to be a carefully managed trial that replicated the conditions under which the ethics classes might be offered. That is, the classes were to be offered only to those students who had *already* opted out of SRE. What in fact occurred was that ethics was offered to all children in the chosen schools prior to any choice for or against SRE. The trial of these classes was mishandled from the beginning. However, the issue attracted an enormous amount of heat. Especially in the inner west of Sydney, the arrival of the ethics course was heralded as the end for SRE and enthusiastically endorsed by local P&C committees even before the trial had been completed.

The Keneally government, under pressure in inner-city seats from the stridently secular Greens and facing massive electoral losses, eventually announced that it would seek to roll out the ethics curriculum as an alternative to SRE in 2011. This was despite vigorous opposition to the plan from the churches, led in the main by Sydney Anglicans.

The opposition of Sydney Anglicans to the ethics pilot was unfortunately typical of a pattern that has been established over the last few decades. It was indicative of an ongoing failure to read the mood of the public and an instinctive defensiveness of a place in the social order that was a century out of date. That the Church was not willing to even negotiate over this issue brought forth frustrated tirades from parents on local talk back radio and in other media. The strident, ill-informed,

---

2. I am speaking from my own experience of attending a multicultural inner city public school in Sydney in the 1970s and 80s. Catholic, Protestant, and Orthodox Scripture classes accounted for the overwhelming majority of children, leaving only a few students to go to the library. Provision for Islamic SRE was not then as widespread as it is now and would have picked up some of the remaining children.

and often misleading reaction to the new ethics program made it look as if the Anglican Church was more interested in protecting its own privileged patch than it was in promoting the welfare of the community it was seeking to serve.

Sydney Anglican leaders had good grounds to complain that the way the "trial" had been conducted was shambolic. The parliamentary processes were not good, especially given that SRE had been specifically and clearly protected by the 1990 Education Act. Sydney Anglicans were also justified in noting that the P&C—dominated as it is by an adamantly secular and socially-progressive agenda—had made the introduction of these classes into something of a mission. Local P&Cs were provided with pre-written motions and instructed in how to bring them to pass unamended. There is no doubt that the introduction of the ethics classes were, in the minds of some parents at least, a strategy to end the availability of SRE classes in government schools altogether.

However, the Sydney Anglican response to the issue was unfortunately representative of an often catastrophic relationship Sydney Anglicans have had with the media in their city over more than three decades. Over the lifetimes of most people in the demographic now aged forty-five and younger, it would be possible to say that the media profile of Sydney Anglicans has been consistently and overwhelmingly negative, defensive, and self-protective. For a Generation Xer, now the parent of a primary school-aged child, there has never been a time when the local Anglican church was not represented in the media as beset by internal wrangling, concerned for trivialities more than realities, and desperate to stall its slide into oblivion. That is the narrative they know.

Despite the stated desire to be missionaries of the gospel of Jesus to their own city, Sydney Anglicans have not been able to recover from the loss of social standing that almost all social institutions have felt since the 1960s. They have acted as if the media owed them a respectful hearing, and as if any attack on them by the media was as a result of a plot of social liberals to send them spiraling into decline. This is not of course to justify or to deny the presence of inept and incompetent reporting by journalists who increasingly have no idea about religious matters at all. What it does reveal is that, like all religious groups at the beginning of the twenty-first century, the diocese of Sydney has to counter the impression that its chief interest is really the maintenance of its own privilege and the defense of its own way of life. They have been quick to blame the alleged agenda of the local media for their failure to communicate their positive vision.

But the signs of a change in this attitude are emerging. My purpose in this chapter is to explore the relationship of Sydney Anglicans to the world outside their churches. What are the underlying causes of the way in which they have related to society and government?

A Holy Huddle?

To proclaim the gospel of Jesus Christ in brutal old Sydney town has never been easy. Nevertheless, the early evangelical leaders saw themselves as responsible not only to win souls but to build "a wholesome society, in which the Worship of God was the center from which human beings and human society would be rebuilt, reformed and rejuvenated."[3] The second chaplain to the colony, Rev. Samuel Marsden, became known as "the flogging parson" because of his over-zealous administration of his weekday duties as magistrate. Despite his evident enthusiasm to preach the good news in New South Wales and also in New Zealand, he became perhaps not unreasonably diverted by the task of building and maintaining social order in a hostile and fragile environment.

His successors likewise felt the combination of inertia and hostility to the gospel wearisome. In his study of Sydney Anglicanism from 1885 to 1914, former lecturer at Moore College Bill Lawton argued that the Sydney Anglicans of that period felt under pressure from the advance of secularism. As they had since the founding of the colony, churchmen noted and bemoaned the loss of respect for Sabbath observation, the prevalence of drunkenness, and threats to traditional patterns of marriage as symptomatic of the decline in the Church's influence on social order. In response to this felt crisis, Lawton argued that local Anglican leaders such as the then principal of Moore College the Welshman Nathanael Jones came to focus their attention not on society but on the "little flock"—the small gathering of believers who were waiting deliverance from the trials and tribulations of the world. They were influenced in this by Brethrenism and the revivalism characteristic of the evangelicalism of the period. As Lawton writes:

---

3. Bolt, "The Two Reverend Messrs. Cowper," 28.

> The religion of these evangelicals was essentially introspective and futurist, fearful of the social and ideological changes taking place around them. Intuitionism combined with millennialism to inhibit their developing a coherent social theory. By concentrating exclusively on ends and goals, Moore College fashioned a clergy whose sole task was to interpret the mind of God to the people of God, but who failed to interpret that mind to a secularized society.[4]

In this period (according to Lawton) retreat from the world was certainly preferable to accommodation to it.

For Lawton, the teaching about the last things—eschatology—explains the increasing defensiveness of local church pronouncements on social issues. Eschatology inevitably leads to questions about the nature of present social order and the role of the Christian church in it. Jones and others taught a form of premillennialism shaped by the thought of the well know Irish preacher John Nelson Darby (1800–1882). For Darby, Scripture was an essentially prophetic book which describes humanity as being progressively dealt with by God in a series of "dispensations." Each dispensation begins with a divinely appointed task that comes with a promise of blessing and ends with an act of divine judgment. In the present dispensation, that of the church, we are to live following the judgment of God on Israel for its hardness of heart and in the light of the expectation that God will restore the kingdom to Israel. The task of the Christian evangelist is to call people *out* of the fallen and disgraced world and into the church—to become one of the truly converted, spiritual gathering of believers. Failing to keep society Christian by legal means or by persuasion in the press, the evangelicals prayed for the coming of revival instead.

A case study from this period was the church's response to the Divorce Extension Bills which were proposals for liberalizing the divorce laws. While in 1886 there was intense debate about the issue of divorce, by the late 1880s, the local churchmen seemed to have retreated. Society's unwillingness to respond to the Bible's authority on this issue seemed to take the wind out of their sails. The intervention of the clergy on this matter had not endeared them to the public: "The daily press, and particularly the Sydney Morning Herald, responded at first cautiously and deferentially but soon editorials began a hostile attack on

---

4. Lawton, *The Better Time to Be*, 89.

the churchmen's lack of compassion and their legalistic concern for semantics."[5]

The advancing tide of secularism was met by an attempt to use the law as an instrument to bring about conformity to the will of God. However when it became apparent that a gap was opening up between Christian standards and the standards of the society at large, Sydney Anglicans (as Lawton argues it) turned their attention back to the "little flock" as a community where divine law could certainly be maintained.

Lawton the historian writes, "Sydney evangelical Anglicanism drew upon the Brethren doctrines of the church as 'gathered community' and the Bible as a record of unfulfilled prophecy. The denomination developed a futurist eschatology in which the local 'gathered' community of Christians was seen as the proleptic expression of the heavenly Church."[6] But this is also evidence of Lawton the contemporary (i.e., 1990) churchman and commentator. Throughout his book Lawton shows himself convinced that this pattern of retreat and defense against the rising tide of secularism driven by a certain eschatology and ecclesiology is characteristic of present day Sydney Anglicanism. His purpose is not merely of antiquarian interest but (like many historians) to critique the present by uncovering a genealogy of theological ideas and tribal instincts. Unfortunately, he makes this case only by inference and not so much by evidence. In order to be convincing, he would have to show that even though premillennial theology and Brethren piety has been completely repudiated by Sydney Anglicans since at least the 1950s, their impress on the Sydney Anglican mindset is still in evidence.[7] Lawton doesn't carry out this tracing of connections explicitly. Were they to be drawn, the lines of connection between the two phases of Sydney Anglican history would be complex and would have to be traced over six decades or more. It would have to account for continuity, when there has been an explicit departure from the ethos of Jones and his followers. There are in fact significant differences between the Brethren view of the church and the doctrine taught by Knox and Robinson. Yet it is worth asking if the defensiveness that Lawton describes has entirely disappeared.

5. Ibid., 156.
6. Ibid., 211.
7. Particularly, as we have seen, since Biblical Theology of the kind Robinson and Goldsworthy taught is explicitly contrary to the dispensationalist view of Scripture.

Big Billy and Beyond

The inference to be drawn from Lawton's argument is that an emphasis on discontinuous and futurist eschatology has had an impact on the way in which Anglicans from Sydney have responded to the rising tide of secularism since the 1960s. What I would like to show is that, while Sydney's Anglicans have not always responded well to the challenges of the new secularism, they were not in fact given to the kind of world-abandonment supposedly characteristic of them in the late nineteenth century.

The period of secularization following the 1960s does indeed have some strong echoes of the late nineteenth century. In between these two eras was the high-water mark of church influence in Australian, and in Sydney especially. In the midst of the Great Depression, Sydney Anglicans like the extraordinary R. B. S. Hammond (1870–1946) at St. Barnabas' Broadway distinguished themselves in remarkable service of the poor. The 1950s in particular was a time in which Australian society seemed more congenial to the influence of the church than it had been previously.

This was demonstrated by the dramatic impact of the Billy Graham crusade of 1959—an event that had all the appearance of the dawn of a new glorious age of Christian social influence through the work of the Holy Spirit in the hearts of the thousands of people who went forward in Sydney and Melbourne. More than 130,000 people made a commitment to Christ—a figure which represents nearly 2 percent of the Australian population at the time. Evangelical historian Stuart Piggin makes the case from the figures of the Australian Bureau of Statistics to show that there was a drop in alcohol consumption, extra-marital births, and crime statistics during that time—signs, as far as he is concerned, that here was a genuine revival.[8] Yet what looked like the herald of the new day turned out to be the evening star. The Graham crusade, at which a generation of the diocese of Sydney's future leader-

---

8. Number of convictions for all crimes doubled between 1950 and 1959 (population rose by 25%), but in 1960, 1961, and 1962 the number of convictions "remained fairly constant," resuming the upward trend in the late 60s. There was a 10% reduction in alcohol sales in 1960-61. Piggin notes: "The Crusades do appear to have modified social behaviour and yet this is only evident in the annual statistics" (Piggin, "Billy Graham in Australia, 1959," 25–26.

ship encountered Jesus Christ himself in a profound and life-changing way, coincided with a renewed impetus for secularization and liberalization in Australian society.

It would be impossible to understate the scale of the social changes that have occurred in a single generation and which have direct impact on the church's relationship with society. Anglicanism carries within its DNA an expectation that it is part of the social order and that it contributes to social cohesion. And yet along with other institutions that played this role in the old Australia, the church's influence was now under attack. Australia's development as a society of leisure had a lot to do with it; whereas once the churches were the hub of the local community's social life, there were now many alternative ways to make use of the freedom afforded by Sunday. The sexual liberation and the rise of feminism have been well-documented to the point of cliché. Successively, the churches failed to halt changes to laws providing for Sunday trading, no-fault divorce, later pub closing times, more gambling and casinos, the right to abortion, rights for de facto marriages, homosexual practice, and the removal of censorship. Whereas once the local media took a respectful interest in church affairs and sought the opinion of the clergy, it now could and wanted to tell a different story: of the decline and fall of a once mighty and vibrant institution. Attendance at church dropped away, though, somewhat mysteriously, belief in Christian teachings did not.

Observing this rapid loss of influence, it is not surprising that the churches feel somewhat besieged. They cannot keep the society Christianized, so they have sought to maintain their own identity and to negotiate their right to exist within the new social framework. Sydney Anglicans are not unique in this. Along with other churches they have sought to maintain their right to freedom from anti-discrimination laws. The opposition of church groups to the proposal for a Bill of Rights under the Rudd government (2007–2009) was largely justified on the grounds that such a bill would represent an opportunity for secularists to place churches under the anti-discrimination laws.[9] Instead of con-

---

9. For example, Jim Wallace of the Australian Christian Lobby was reported as saying: "A bill or charter of rights can . . . be a Trojan horse for minority agendas which have failed to make the grade with voters" (http://www.journeyonline.com.au/showArticle.php?articleId=1549). There were indeed good reasons to be suspicious of the Bill of Rights on a number of grounds, in my opinion. What is of interest here is the arguments to which the churches appealed.

sidering what an opportunity for good the affirmation of human rights might mean for the vulnerable, the churches bemoaned the potential loss of their own privileged separation.

But Sydney Anglicans have not been inert in those decades. Far from it: they have pursued their understanding of mission with extraordinary vigor in those times. Sydney Anglicans faced their loss of social influence in the law and in the running of people's workaday lives by reminding each other that that this was not what the call to make disciples of all nations meant anyhow. Perhaps more quickly than other Anglicans, these evangelical Anglicans realized that they depended on a divine work for the transformation of individuals. They did not become more politicized, but less. Where other Anglicans jumped on the bandwagon of progressivist social change, Sydney Anglicans saw this as craven capitulation to the spirit of the age. They did not pursue a reactionary politics, however. They pinned their hopes on evangelism and building the church through recruiting a generation of clergy.

Billy Graham was invited back in 1968 and 1979 in an effort to recapture the atmosphere of the halcyon days of 1959. These crusades were in themselves indicators of just how much had changed in a few short years. Whereas in 1959 the organizers could bus in thousands of nominal churchgoers in hats and gloves, in 1968 and 1979 this was no longer a reality. In 1959 youth groups were full of young people for whom confirmation or baptism was a rite of passage into adult society. Only the children of churchgoers remained in confirmation groups by the 1970s. The conversions of 1959 had not arrested the slide into de-Christianization. The evangelists were now coming to a society for whom church involvement was a fading memory. Baptisms, church weddings, and funerals conducted by clergy would in time become exceptions rather than the habit of Sydneysiders.

Sydney Anglicans pursued another strategy with better success—university ministry. This was not new for evangelical Anglicans, of course—their presence at the leading British universities through the InterVarsity Fellowship (now the UCCF) was longstanding. The Sydney University Evangelical Union had long been the recruiting ground for Sydney Anglican leaders, lay and clerical. By the early 1970s, however, the EU had become distracted by a variety of social causes and had lost numbers. At the University of New South Wales, however, the new chaplain, Phillip Jensen, was beginning a ministry of evangelism, bible exposition, and recruitment for ministry that would reach its height by the early 1990s. By the late 1980s, the Sydney University EU had likewise experienced a remarkable renovation of purpose, with evangelistic missions in 1977, 1980, 1981, 1984, 1986, 1988, 1989, and 1991.[10] The national student movement, AFES, rapidly came to be dominated by graduates of the UNSW programs. Moore College's numbers doubled in a decade. That this occurred when churches everywhere—and especially Anglican churches elsewhere in Australia—were in rapid decline made the achievement all the more remarkable.

The key to the advancement of the gospel in the secular age was to recruit young people for full-time ministry from the university campuses. The Ministry Training Scheme (MTS), started at the University of New South Wales in the early 1980s, invited young university graduates to embark on a two-year ministry apprenticeship at the university prior to theological training. This trainee period would prove to be *the* formative experience for a generation of Sydney Anglican clergy, university workers, and missionaries.

As a scheme for ensuring the evangelical character and the strength of churches and other institutions it was, and continues to be, very successful. It produced competent, energetic, and well-trained clergy and church leaders with a clear sense of what to do. Other theological colleges around the country relied (and still rely) on handfuls of part-time students and middle-aged ordinands. Sydney's ordinands were well under that median age and had signed up for a life time of arduous work in the Lord's vineyards. It produced churches that were (and are) well taught.

But was this focus on the ministry the result of an underlying eschatology of separation between this world and the next? Valuing gospel work over secular work was indeed a decision for the eternal rather than the ephemeral, because "the time is short" (1 Cor 7:29). This authentically biblical theology has enormous power as a critique of a this-worldly, middle-class idolatry of careers in the hothouse environment

10. The president of the Sydney University Evangelical Union Adrian Lane twisted evangelist John Chapman's arm to come to the 1977 mission, adopting the model of the Vietnam war protests on the front lawn. Prior to this, the student movement had been inactive in evangelistic missions, as many thought public evangelism was too threatening. "As a consequence [of the success of the Sydney EU mission], the EUs of other Australian universities took up the challenge of public evangelism," resulting in a wave of missions around the country (Orpwood, *Chappo*, 128).

of the university campus. But it is not at all the same as the premillenialism that Lawton observed at the end of the nineteenth century. The note of eschatological urgency was not now offered at the expense of tending to the needs of society as it had been then. Opportunities to do good are still reckoned by the Anglicans of Sydney to be opportunities to do good, whatever the lateness of the eschatological hour.[11]

That being said, the relatively quietist approach of Sydney Anglicans to politics itself should not be seen in isolation from that broader cultural pattern. Christianity in Australia has never been as politicized as it is in the US or even in the UK. There are obvious exceptions such as Daniel Mannix (1864–1963), Roman Catholic archbishop of Melbourne for much of the twentieth century, who openly intervened in political debates amid much controversy. But he is the exception that proves the rule. Sydney Anglicans have, for the most part, looked for a happy collaboration with the state rather than pursued theocratic aims. They have not abandoned hope for social transformation, but they do see its best chance as arising from the preaching of the gospel and the changed hearts that result.

Though Sydney Anglicans were prominent in the Lausanne movement that declared in 1974 that the pursuit of social justice was entirely compatible with preaching the gospel, they were not enthusiastic for political and social ends *per se*. They were in fact strong critics of a kind of Christianity that denied the pressing claims of the coming end of all things and instead become a social gospel.

For Broughton Knox, "social justice" was itself a questionable category. In an article entitled "Social Justice or Compassion" he argued that "the teaching and actions of Jesus nowhere show a concern for "social justice"": "The reason is that the call for social justice springs from envy rather than from compassion . . . Compassion, not social justice, is the motivation for Christian social action . . . Poverty calls for compassion . . . but a Christian is not called on to campaign for a closer equalisation of incomes either within our society, nor for that matter between nation and nation. Christ's gospel is not concerned with equity

---

11. For example, the 1971 Annual Report of the Anglican Home Mission Society, Sydney (now Anglicare) which listed that it employed three hundred staff and turned over $169,000, reminded the diocese that "Jesus's ministry was never divorced from everyday life." Likewise, in 1989 it asserted that "The Word of God and the Work of God are two sides of one coin."

but with relationships."¹² It was a provocative point to make, since the language of social justice had become a nostrum even within the evangelical movement. It was not an empty academic point, either: Knox was personally and actively compassionate towards the poor. I lived in the principal's residence at Moore College in the years following Knox's retirement and can recall the stream of homeless men that would come to the door asking to see the "padre" from whom they had received help in the past.

But the compassion that the gospel requires does not, in Knox's view, mean a mandate to pursue social change. When it came to writing about race, Knox was initially supportive of a policy of just and peaceable segregation. In Australia, that meant provision for the Aboriginal peoples of separate land on generous terms—something that Australian law is still seeking to facilitate as a matter of justice. In South Africa, it meant that, in principle, apartheid was not an evil system. Its application certainly could be accused of imbalance and injustice but not the system as an idea in and of itself.[13]

Australia's political culture is robustly democratic and so a quietist stance is not in itself problematic for the most part. Other groups tend to take up the cudgels against social injustices, and there are few issues in which the lines are sharply drawn. However, the cost of this passivity can be observed in the history of the Church of England in South Africa, with whom the diocese of Sydney has had historic links. CESA was not a racist church, and it has long had black and white congregations and bishops. It did not provide a theological justification for the apartheid policies of the South African government. However, in the aftermath of the apartheid years, Bishop Frank Retief of CESA made this submission, in 1997, to a hearing of the Truth and Reconciliation Commission:

> When the government made legislation that accorded with our moral or biblical understanding, we supported them. However, on the great issue of justice for all, we were often insensitive. We had not made the connection between gospel and society . . . We

12. Knox, *D. Broughton Knox*, 3:165.

13. Ibid., 3:194. Knox carefully argued that Abraham's separation from his nephew Lot should be the model. Abraham offered the best land to Lot, not the worst. He wrote: "It is not the policy of geographical separateness that Christians should condemn, but any injustice in applying the policy . . . but genuine injustice needs to be fearlessly condemned."

were witnesses to how the Bible and its message can be misused to support an evil ideology. National government used the Bible to support its policies, to give the impression that they were a Christian government. But then so did some liberation theologians who finally supported violence as a means of continuing the struggle . . Where we have been negligent, careless and insensitive to biblical injunctions and mandates as we have been, may the Lord graciously forgive us . . . The fact that the Bible was used in the past to condone injustice does not mean its true message may be ignored today . . . It is our belief that this day and hour calls for men and women of conviction and integrity to apply the message of the Bible more accurately and faithfully to our emerging society . . .[14]

This is a courageous, impressive, and moving statement from a cousin of the Sydney diocese recognizing that the strategy of political withdrawal was a mistake for biblical Christians in South Africa, but recognizing also that it was not the Bible itself that was to blame. Retief's theological convictions are the same as Sydney's, and he has often spoken in the pulpits of Sydney. What he confesses is the terrible reality of becoming unable to say anything about the presence of a real evil. Compassion is not nearly enough.

Relating as the church to the world is a complicated business. Like all churches, Sydney's Anglicans have not always got it right. However, it was simply not the case that a theology of world-denial was in operation here. The Biblical Theology of Robinson presses Sydney Anglicans to a more nuanced doctrine of creation than that. The priority given to evangelism over social justice is not a negation of the pressing needs of the world. It is in fact a decision about what is best to do about the plight of the world and what will be most effective to promote the good of society. Having said this is not to claim that Sydney's Anglicans have always done as much as they should have, or that they have always got the business of dealing with the world right.

Connecto9 and Saying "Yes" to the World

When Peter Jensen—himself a convert from the '59 Billy Graham crusade—became archbishop in 2001, he quickly announced that the first

14. Retief, "Church of England in South Africa."

decade of the new millennium would be devoted to the proclamation of the gospel. He named an audacious target—to have 10 percent of the population of Sydney in Bible-believing churches. The target was meant to be the catalyst for change in diocesan structures and to give energy to the parishes to be innovative and courageous. If the naming of the 10 percent target was often criticized, it was because it was frequently misunderstood

Things did not go entirely according to the plan, at least humanly speaking. Looking back from the vantage point of 2012 it is apparent that change has been slow and momentum has been hard to gather. Devastating financial losses in the 2008 global financial crisis have crippled much of the diocesan infrastructure. The most significant event of the past ten years has been the Connect09 mission. Planned to run exactly fifty years after Billy Graham's first Sydney visit, it was almost the exact antithesis of that event. There was no "big" overseas speaker brought in. There were no stadiums booked or mass events planned. Other than endorsement of the Bible Society's *Jesus—All About Life* campaign, there was no mass media advertising. Distribution of the gospel of Luke in massive numbers was central to the strategy.

But in two ways Connect09 represented a return to the true focus of Sydney Anglicans—in the first instance back to the parishes and away from the diocesan center, and second, back to the community itself. "Connect" was a brilliantly chosen slogan because it invited the parishes to start rebuilding the bridges that had been burnt in the 60s and 70s. It was not a strategy for revival on the old model that depended in large part on a Christianized culture. A well-meaning nostalgia for those days was not going to make much headway in cynical post-Christendom Sydney. Instead, the emphasis was on community. The executive director of Connect09, Rev. Andrew Nixon, wrote these telling words in 2008:

> I spoke to a man the other day who does market research (focus groups and interviews) with a wide range of people: what they like and don't like; what they think and feel about various things. He said that overwhelmingly what people want more than anything else is belonging: to fit in and be accepted; to have a role; to matter to other people. A place where they belong. Yet, he said, paradoxically, the places in society where people can find belonging—like tennis clubs, service clubs, churches, boy scouts and girl guides—are all in massive decline . . . We have bigger

BBQs and TVs than ever before, and as we huddle round them we yearn for community; we yearn to belong. If what this man says is true, our suburbs are full of people who long deep down to have what we have . . . How can we build that community beyond the doors of church and let it overflow into our streets and suburbs where it is so desperately needed?[15]

The note of triumphalism is muted here, with recognition that the task of preaching the gospel in contemporary secular Australia is onerous. A "magic bullet" approach of wheeling in the well-known overseas evangelist is not, humanly speaking, the way in which Australia will be reached with the gospel of Jesus.

The Connect09 strategy could represent a watershed moment in the Sydney diocese's relationship to the community it lives to serve. It offers this potential in a number of ways. First of all, it hands the keys to the car back to the laity as the frontline of engagement with those outside the church. Clericalism was only ever going to be a saving strategy—it could never be a plan for growth. Connect09 liberated the parishioners of Sydney to think creatively about how they might reach their neighbors. This takes the pressure off the clergy of whom so much was expected and in whom so much was invested—and empowers them to be more effective.

Second, parishes were encouraged to see themselves as part of the local community and not merely separate from it. In many instances, the Anglican parish joins with the local primary school in being the last remaining noncommercial community organization present in a suburb or town. The effects of contemporary urbanization have wrought a devastating cost in social dislocation. Church buildings themselves stand against this tide—something that local communities themselves often recognize. The massive sandstone gothic of St. Andrew's Summer Hill was even adopted by the local municipal council as its symbol for the area.

Third, the massive social welfare arm of the diocese, Anglicare, has begun to be much better integrated with parishes. Anglicare has been a remarkable engine of connection with the community at need, supporting the parishes of the diocese rather than working around them and even unbeknownst to them. Further cooperation with Moore College

15. http://www.sydneyanglicans.net/ministry/connect09/community_the_key_to_connection/

could also enable some serious thinking to be done about community, social justice, and care for the poor from within the convictional world of Sydney Anglicanism.

Fourth, Connect09 reminded Sydney Anglicans that the front line of ministry is always the parish church. The focus on the central institution has an unreality about it that is countered by the flesh and blood presence of the communities of God's people dotted throughout the vast urban area. It is here that the gospel of Jesus Christ touches down and starts to make sense to those who do not yet know him. The gospel as it is embodied in the lives of those who believe it can be seen week by week in the gatherings of God's people.

Fifth, Connect09 asks some challenging theological questions. It demands a recalibration of Sydney's theological convictions to suit the requirements of mission in the contemporary world. As always, Sydney Anglicanism's theological leaders will not abandon their commitment to the authority of Scripture or to the centrality of the blood of Christ given for sins. However, as Archbishop Jensen pointed out in his 2010 synod address, a robust theological anthropology is required for the new day. The rise of a militant "new" atheism has re-exposed some thorny theological problems, such as the nature of faith in its relationship to reason. The changing world demands an ecclesiology that is more porous and less defensive. If Sydney Anglicans are genuinely to connect with their neighbors, they will have to address the questions that are now on the table.

Despite all these promising signs, the challenge remains for Sydney Anglicans: will they be able to overcome the defensiveness that has marked their stance on public issues (such as the debate over ethics classes) over the last few decades and move onto a more positive and even prophetic footing? Can they relate to the media not as another group determined to mark out its territory and defend its right to exist but as a community genuinely committed to the public good? Can they behave in public as if they really do believe in the supreme Lordship of Christ and that they have nothing to fear? If their gospel is the power and wisdom of God himself, then there is no need to act from insecurity. If fear is the basis from which Sydney Anglicans speak then they will find themselves talking only to each other and becoming increasingly incomprehensible to those on the outside. Moore College theologian Andrew Cameron has written persuasively that there are points at which the church needs to say not just "no" to the world, but also "yes."[16]

To be a genuinely gospel-centered church engaged with the civil body politic is not as straightforward as it sounds. However, the martyrs of the early church demonstrate that it is possible to stand fearlessly and loyally before Caesar's representative and witness truly for Jesus Christ. This was possibly the most effective mission strategy ever devised.

---

16. Cameron, "How to Say Yes to the World."

nine

Sydney Anglicans and the Ministry of Women

A Line In the Sand

At the Sydney synod of 2006, Rev. Chris Albany, the rector of South Hurstville, attempted to put forward a bill supporting the ordination of women to the priesthood. Since 1992, women had been serving as priests in almost all of the other dioceses of the Anglican Church of Australia. It had by 2007 ceased to be a novelty. Two women bishops were to be consecrated only the following year.

This was by some accounts the fifteenth time that the issue had come before the synod since the ordination of women was first touted in 1977. In 1987, Sydney had consented to the ordination of women as deacons but had not progressed further. In 2006, the reaction from Sydney's synod was overwhelming. It decided that they did not even want Albany's bill discussed. About 70 percent of lay members (235)—the elected representatives of ordinary pew-sitters around the diocese—voted against while 85 percent of clergy (165) also voted no. In fact, this represented an increase in the no vote since 1996 and even since 1992. It was clear that there was no way that the synod was going to budge on this matter.

If there is any single issue with which Sydney's Anglicans have found themselves identified, it is surely the matter of the ordination of women to the priesthood. That Anglicans in other dioceses and the wider community are bewildered and even appalled by the failure of Anglicans in Sydney to allow complete gender equality in ministry is actually proof to them of the justness of their cause. Christians are surely called to be different to the world that surrounds them; here is an area in which this group of Christians, with a surprising consensus between laity and clergy and male and female members, has not allowed social pressure and a Whiggish view of history to dictate the shape of their faith. For Sydney Anglicans, this issue is primarily about the authority of Scripture. In fact, by appealing to grounds other than Scripture, such as the work of the Holy Spirit in history and culture, the opponents of Sydney have further entrenched Sydney's opposition to the innovation.

I have in this chapter a difficult and perhaps even impossible task—namely, to give an apology for the Sydney position when there are those who find it disgraceful and even unchristian. The shocking incomprehensibility of Sydney's position to many people can be broken down into three questions on which they have fundamentally different answers: is leadership by equals thinkable? Is role by design thinkable? Is self-sacrificial authority possible? On all these questions the spirit of our age has come, through bitter experience, to a resounding "no." Many Sydney Anglicans, from their reading of Scripture, say "yes." I am not asking for, or expecting, concurrence. I would like to convince the skeptics that this is a position of deep conviction and not merely an excuse for chauvinism. But at the same time I would like to call the diocese of Sydney, including myself, to a deeper integrity about the ministry and treatment of women.

Is Leadership By Equals Thinkable?

Evangelicals do not hold to a primarily hierarchical view of humanity, or of the church, or of the ministry. They are insistent on the profound equality of all human beings in God's eyes—who will be equally judged by him and to whom Christ equally comes. In the nineteenth century, evangelicals were in the vanguard of the movement for female enfranchisement, just as they had been at the forefront of the fight against slavery.[1] They note that most ministry in the New Testament church is carried out amongst "one-another"; that gifts of prophecy come to both men and women (Acts 2; 1 Cor 11); and that the orders of ministry such as they are described in the New Testament do not convey special

---

1. Bebbington, *The Dominance of Evangelicalism*, 203–5.

powers or superior spiritual status. But does the existence of orders of leadership undermine this essential equality?

The Anglican Church has been for most of its history a child of its British culture, and so habitually hierarchical and clericalized. When in the 1960s the laity were admitted to the public ministries of the church such as reading, praying, service leading, and so on, evangelicals warmly endorsed the change as being truer to the gospel of Christ. In retrospect, it was inevitable that the question of the elevation of women to all the ministries of the church from which they had been up till that moment denied access would prove a more troublesome prospect. Unlike Anglo-Catholics, evangelicals do not believe that the priest has some special spiritual status by dint of his ordination. The argument that Christ only chose male apostles and that therefore the Church ought only to ordain male priests carries precisely no weight with Sydney's evangelicals, especially as for evangelicals eldership is not about presiding at the Eucharist. It is primarily because here was a matter on which Scripture is not silent.

The text which is decisive on the issue in the Sydney Anglican way of thinking is 1 Tim 2:11–15 that reads: "A woman should learn in quietness and full submission. I do not permit a woman to teach or to assume authority over a man; she must be quiet. For Adam was formed first, then Eve. And Adam was not the one deceived; it was the woman who was deceived and became a sinner. But women will be saved through childbearing—if they continue in faith, love and holiness with propriety."[2]

This passage does not speak about ordination per se. The apostle here addresses a particular activity—the business of authoritative teaching in the gathering. And he differentiates between the roles he gives to men and women in this activity. He does so by appealing to Genesis 2–3. Applying the principles drawn from this passage to the particular forms of ministry that they have inherited, Sydney's Anglicans have chosen, through the synod, to restrict the role of "priest" or "presbyter" to men, since this role most closely matches the role of authoritative teacher.

But there is also a deeper theological conviction about the nature of church itself that provides a backdrop to the Sydney Anglican teaching

---

2. That is not say that it is the only relevant text or that the entire Bible is read through the lens of this text.

on this subject. It is, as Broughton Knox said, that "The Christian congregation should reflect the structure of the Christian home."[3] In a piece dated around 1973, Knox insisted that it was the context of ministry in the congregation that made gender such an important issue. There was nothing in terms of ability that might prevent a woman from carrying out any of the functions of the ministry. They were obviously no more or less than capable to lead services, celebrate communion, visit the sick, and bury the dead than their brothers. But these ministries take place in a congregation that is not a business meeting or a social club but rather has the character of a family. In the New Testament, the ministers are appointed from among household leaders (1 Tim 3:1–12; Titus 1:5–6) and part of their qualification for leadership in the church is the effectiveness and integrity of their leadership in the home as husbands and fathers. The New Testament in several passages speaks about the relationship of husbands and wives, not naming an essential hierarchy between them, but depicting a pattern of leadership-through-service, and submission as a response.

At this point, Knox does speak of hierarchy and refers his readers to 1 Cor 11:7–11. He is not persuaded that this passage is merely a reflection of first century culture, "though the consequence of this principle will vary in different cultures."[4] There is an order outlined in this passage from God to Christ to man and thence to woman. Between the man and the woman, however, the order is marked by a thoroughgoing interdependence in a way in which you could not say that the divine is dependent on the human. The note of hierarchy is muted by a profound mutuality and equality. It is not an order that is exercised in "lording it" and a corresponding servility but is rather marked by sacrificial service and response. This is what is known as "headship"—in recognition of the word which is used in 1 Cor 11.

Now, there's a quite subtle intermediate step that is often missed by proponents of the "headship" view. Male headship of the family is not simply transposed onto the church. The head of the church, after all, is not the male minister who leads it—it is Jesus Christ. The elder is not the "father" of the congregation. If anything, the church's internal relationships are characterized as fraternal—the mothers and daughters, fathers and sons are now in a sibling relationship in Christ. Male

3. Knox, *D. Broughton Knox*, 2:208.
4. Ibid., 2:207.

leadership of the church is desirable because it doesn't overthrow male headship of the family. As Knox explains: "relationships between men and women in the congregation should not contradict relationships of the home."[5]

Application of the principles of headship and submission in church order complicates things further. Amongst conservative Sydney Anglicans there is quite a lot of difference of opinion on how these convictions might be expressed. Some would hesitate to have women lead services or mixed Bible study groups. Others would be in favor of women preaching, though not as the rector of a parish. Since women were admitted to the order of deacon in 1987, some parishes have had female preaching in mixed congregations for more than two decades.[6] To a greater or lesser extent, what needs to be realized is the inexact fit between the church of the first century and the Anglican church of the twenty-first. Anglican ordination and contemporary church leadership models do not merely replicate or signify the same thing as the biblical practice. Unfortunately, there are those who do not notice this gap and who assume that their application of the principle is a direct application of the teaching of Scripture. Knox himself admitted to more flexibility in practice than is sometimes imagined of him. In the early 1970s he wrote this intriguing sentence: "The New Testament does not consider the anomaly when Christian men are incompetent, ill-prepared or unwilling to discharge the teaching ministry. In this anomalous situation it may well be that what is normal must give place to what is beneficial!"[7] Knox was clearly not an absolutist in the sense that he held that the principle he put forward must be held whatever the circumstances. However strongly he felt the command was made, that he granted this exception indicates that was clearly not some kind of moral issue for him,

Those who oppose and criticize Sydney's position on women's ordination often resort to amateur psychology in order to demonstrate that this conviction about what Scripture teaches is unreal or that it is a pretext for what amounts to the expression of a kind of collective

---

5. Ibid., 2:202.

6. Prior to this, women were permitted to give an "address," primarily to allow returning missionaries the chance to speak to congregations. This was not considered "preaching."

7. Knox, *D. Broughton Knox*, 2:245.

psychopathy.[8] This is rather typical of a kind of postmodern power-critique that cannot believe even what someone says about their own views and why they hold them. Its logic is reductive ("you might say X, but really it is just because of Y") and it proves nothing. After all, it is quite possible to believe the truth for the wrong reasons. Certainly, plain old sexism exists within the diocese of Sydney (as it does everywhere) and this theology can be used as a pretext to justify it. But it is also the case that ordaining women to the priesthood and consecrating them as bishops has not eradicated misogyny either. The fact of the matter is that Sydney Anglicans are by and large people of conviction and that this is their sincerely-held conviction.

Arianism Considered—The Giles Controversy

The thinkability of "leadership by equals" came under direct attack in the late 1990s and early 2000s. The chief antagonist of Sydney on this occasion was the Australian Anglican theologian Kevin Giles. A graduate of Moore College, Giles has spent most of his ministry working in evangelical parishes in the dioceses of Adelaide and Melbourne. What prompted Giles to enter the fray was the publication of the Sydney Diocese Doctrine Commission Report on the Trinity.

There's a bit of backstory to the controversy. In the mid-1990s, the then archbishop of Sydney Harry Goodhew called together a discussion day on the issue of the ordination of women at Trinity Grammar School. At that day, and much to the surprise of those present, the leading advocate of women's ordination, Dr. Stuart Piggin, brought the radical equality of the persons of the Trinity forward as an argument for a complete equality of roles between the genders in all aspects. He argued:

> Paul argues no priority of male and female and no subordination, only a fundamental equality. This is all consistent with Paul's idea of headship which is based on his understanding of

---

8. The most egregious case of this was Archbishop Peter Carnley's speech to general synod in 1987, who described opponents of the ordination of women as driven by "psycho-spiritual" motives, owing to absent fathers during WWII and even asked "Had too many mothers supervised their sons' baths for too long?" Muriel Porter, who agrees with this assessment, offers some amateur psychologizing of her own (Porter, *Sydney Anglicans and the Threat to World Anglicanism*, 114).

> the Godhead. That God is the head of Christ means that the "Son is eternally begotten of the Father," or "of the same stuff as" and therefore equal to God. By analogy, the female is "of the same stuff as" and therefore equal to the male. For, in creation, God made us human, male and female. There is no order of subordination in this understanding of headship . . . Subordination is a matter of the freedom of the will, not of some imposed order: it is voluntary and mutual, and for us in the Church, it is "out of reverence for Christ."[9]

This was, to those listening, a new dimension in the argument, now going beyond mere exegesis of the relevant texts and anchoring the order of human relationships in the character of God. The stakes had been considerably raised. Some may vaguely have recalled comments by Broughton Knox along these lines some decades before, but since in Sydney the debate had taken place on the exegesis of texts and not on the theological substructures, this appeal to the Trinity seemed to come out of the blue.

In response, Archdeacon Narelle Jarrett framed a question for the Sydney Diocese Doctrine Commission asking it to consider the matter of the doctrine of the Trinity in regards to the competing models for male and female roles in ministry and marriage.

The Doctrine Commission's report was not a lengthy treatise, but nevertheless it concluded that a functional subordination in the Trinity was not excluded by the fundamental equality of the persons. This was its final paragraph:

> The Doctrine Commission agrees that the concept of "subordination" has significant implications. It concludes, furthermore, that the concept of "functional subordination," of equality of essence with order in relation, represents the long-held teaching of the church, and that it is securely based on the revelation of the Scriptures. This teaching should, therefore, determine our commitment both to the equality of men and women in creation and salvation, and also to appropriately biblical expressions of the functional difference between men and women in home and church.

The commission was at pains to distinguish its position from "subordinationism"—that teaching that became notorious in church history in the Arian controversy of the fourth century. Furthermore, it was

9. Piggin, "Address Given at the Launch of Kevin Giles' Book."

cautious, even reticent, about applying the analogy between trinitarian and human relations. Its claim was not that a pattern of ontological equality with functional subordination was hereby established as a template onto which human relationships could be grafted, but rather that the pattern of equality with subordination in the Godhead certainly meant that such a pattern was intelligible and permissible were it to be established on other grounds. The tactical mistake that the report made was that it continued to use the terminology of "subordination" to describe the differentiation of roles between the genders. Since this was the language used to describe the heresy the church has historically rejected, it would have been better advised to find a more congenial expression. This language proved to be the point at which Giles would aim his rhetorical arsenal.[10]

For his part, Kevin Giles first hit the presses in 2002 with his book *The Trinity and Subordinationism*.[11] Carrying commendations from evangelical luminaries such as the US theologian Millard J. Erickson (1932–), it was a strong denunciation of the Sydney Doctrine Commission, whose report he included in an appendix. They were, Giles claimed, guilty of nothing less than the ancient heresy of Arianism.

Giles's stated aim is to move beyond the "bitter stalemate"[12] that has bogged down the debate over exegesis of the relevant scriptural texts and to show from the overwhelming consensus of the tradition that his opponents have invented a novel interpretation of the Trinity driven solely by the need to justify the "permanent subordination of women" (as he characterizes it—it is not language used by its proponents). The tradition, Giles surmises, will offer a clear line of vindication for his position. This seems like a curious move for an evangelical son of the Reformation to employ—and is perhaps a tacit concession that his side of the debate has far more work to do on the scriptural texts to make them suit his case. Unfortunately for Giles, reading and interpreting the tradition is just as controversial and disputed as the reading of the scriptural texts is. The "bitter stalemate"—if the terms Giles has set for resolution of the issue are accepted—remains.

---

10. Even egalitarian theologian Millard Erickson judges the report "cautious and carefully nuanced" (Erickson, *Who's Tampering with the Trinity?*, 52.
11. Giles, *The Trinity and Subordinationism*.
12. Ibid., 3.

Giles completely overstates what his opponents are claiming for their description of trinitarian relations. He casts the Sydney theologians as so obsessed with the single issue of male headship that they will cynically introduce a novel reading of the doctrine of God in order to justify their misogyny. That is: he accuses his opponents of inventing their trinitarian doctrine on the basis of their anthropological presuppositions. Since the Sydney Doctrine Commission report explicitly denies this move, Giles must be privy by some mysterious means to some knowledge of their mental states of which even they themselves are unaware. He seems to exempt himself the possibility that he may also be liable to the same charge of reading his anthropology onto the Trinity.[13]

Giles's accusation of Arianism has affected the reputation of the Sydney diocese internationally. For example, in *The Cambridge Companion to Evangelical Theology*, UK scholar Elaine Storkey simply repeats verbatim Giles's accusations of trinitarian revisionism.[14] Australian Anglican Primate Archbishop Peter Carnley, who had originally outlined a hierarchical trinitarianism in support of a hierarchy of ministries, saw in Giles's accusation an opportunity too good to miss and so changed his mind, accusing Sydney of Arianism in his 2004 book *Reflections in Glass*.[15]

The problem with being on the receiving end of such extreme criticism is that it makes it hard to think straight about one's own position. Too often the way in which the accuser frames the debate becomes integral to the self-identity of the accused. Sydney Anglicans must see past this danger. They did not, despite what Giles and Storkey allege, derive order in gender relations from a new reading of the Trinity. In fact, Sydney Anglicans are far more likely to seek theological inspiration for their marriage relationships and church roles in the self-sacrifice of

---

13. This is pointed out by Michael Bird and Robert Shillaker. Giles has coined "Giles guideline" which is: "Whenever the Trinity is construed to support a prior belief, then the orthodox doctrine of the Trinity is invariably corrupted and distorted." Bird and Shillaker wryly observe that this must surely apply to Giles himself as much as to his opponents (Bird and Shillaker, "Subordination in the Trinity and Gender Roles," 281).

14. Storkey, "Evangelical Theology and Gender," 171.

15. Carnley, *Reflections in Glass*. A detailed report of the controversy that ensued and a judicious assessment of the book is offered by Tom Frame in ch. 6 of Frame and Treloar, *Agendas for Australian Anglicanism*.

Christ for his church (taking the lead from Paul in Eph 5:25), or in the diverse equality of the genders built into both creation accounts (following Jesus in Mark 10:6). Unlike the more gung-ho North American complementarians,[16] Sydney Anglicans only observe a connection between "subordination" in the eternal Trinity and male/female with the utmost reticence and with all the necessary caveats in place. They most certainly upheld the fundamental ontological equality and interrelation of the persons of the Trinity. What must not happen is for this assertion of fundamental equality and mutual inherence to become a neglected theme in Sydney theological thinking, about God and about men and women, because of the human tendency to major on points of difference rather than points of similarity.

It would be, in my opinion, advisable to revisit the 1999 report and offer some clarifications.[17] The danger of saying more, of course, is that you potentially offer more ammunition to detractors like Giles. However, given the misunderstanding and misreading generated by the 1999 document, it would be well worth conceding that the language of "eternal subordination" used in that piece is a distraction and could be revised without loss of the essential point.[18] Even greater care could be taken in a fresh report to deny that any direct and unqualified analogy, unmediated by the actual texts of Scripture, is being drawn between the trinitarian relations and those of the human genders.[19]

---

16. Ware, "Tampering with the Trinity," 252–3; Schreiner, "Head Coverings, Prophecies and the Trinity," 124–39; Ortlund Jr. "Male-Female Equality and Male Headship: Genesis," 103, all in *Biblical Foundations for Manhood and Womanhood*.

17. In 2004–2005, the Sydney Doctrine Commission indeed met to reconsider their report in the light of correspondence from Giles and Carnley, but determined that there was no need to change the view of the 1999 report. The chairman of the commission, John Woodhouse, wrote to the archbishop that "the Commission is of the opinion that no substantial case has been made that the 1999 Report on the Doctrine of the Trinity is in serious error . . . The Doctrine Commission therefore supports the teaching of the 1999 Report although in the light of subsequent debate it would elaborate some points more fully today and possibly express some matters in clearer language," (cited in Frame and Treloar, *Agendas for Australian Anglicanism*, 156).

18. Bird and Shillaker suggest German theologian Wolfhart Pannenberg's language of "eternal and obedient self-distinction of the Son from the Father" ("The Son Really, Really Is the Son," 259). Robert Letham speaks of a "suitable disposition, a well-arranged constitution" (*The Holy Trinity*, 491).

19. Bird and Shillaker, who find themselves "in essential agreement with the view that the eternal subordination of the Son to the Father is consistent with both the biblical materials and historical orthodoxy," urge a moratorium on the use of the trinitarian

Is It Thinkable that the Genders Are Designed for Different Roles?

Thus far I have addressed the issue of gender relations as if it is merely an in-house theological discussion. Of course this is not the case. The question of differences between the genders and the way in which individuals can best express their masculine and feminine identities is one with which Western culture at large is still contending, with pain and confusion. Kelly Burke, the *Sydney Morning Herald* religion reporter in early 2000s, noted how "laughable, if not downright offensive" the notion of male headship is to most of her readers (and that Sydney Anglicans haven't seemed to notice).[20] At the same time, the pages of her own newspaper daily record the anxiety that our community experiences with regard to gender. More than ever before the issue of gender has become bound up with one's own personal identity. Since the zeitgeist emphasizes the freedom of the individual to self-create, especially over against any prefabricated notion of "roles," the discussion of "headship" is always going to jar with our wider cultural sensibilities. Is "roles by design"—the thought that in specific spheres like family and church life, we shape our unique roles against a broad canvas already painted for us by the creator—thinkable? Undoubtedly there is great latitude afforded to different individuals and cultures to interpret what it means to be woman and man—but are we starting with something more interesting than a blank slate?

Individual freedom brings with it enormous anxiety. If the expression of my maleness or femaleness is not dictated to me by some social order and is something that I have to discover for myself, then an inner resourcefulness and self-awareness is asked of me that I may just not have. That is why, even given the freedom to experiment with how gender is expressed, most men and women conform to contemporary cultural norms of gender. They may not be men like their fathers or women like their mothers, but they are overwhelmingly much the same as their brothers and sisters and friends. The vacuum of anxiety created by individual freedom is quickly filled, that is to say, by social conformity, fashion, and self-help books. The irony is that Western culture is

---

analogy in support of either complementarianism or egalitarianism ("Subordination in the Trinity and Gender Roles," 282).

20. McGillion, *The Chosen Ones*, 143.

filled with numerous tacit rules and conventions that quite strictly govern gendered behavior—even to the extent of, say, determining what drinks a heterosexual man can and cannot order at a bar.

Amidst this confusion and anxiety, Holy Scripture is not an embarrassment but a positive asset for Christians—whatever Kelly Burke's readers might have thought. Evangelical Christians, whatever their view on the role of women in ministry and the home, have in Scripture a way of speaking of the profound and ineradicable sameness and mutuality of the human male and female. Men are not from Mars, and women are not from Venus: they are both very much of the earth, and together image God. The Bible reminds us that we cannot conceive of maleness-without-femaleness or femaleness-without-maleness (1 Cor 11). Scripture gives an explanation, too, of the tension that exists between the sexes in their quest for power over one another (Gen 3:16). The biblical pattern of marriage in terms of husbandly sacrificial love and the wifely response of submission is more than a remedy to this condition—it is an emblem of the gospel of Jesus Christ (Eph 5) in which the transformation of humanity itself is declared.

The label "complementarian" has been given to and claimed by those who believe that the roles we shape for men and women in the church's ministry should somehow express this creation backdrop—often concluding that authoritative teaching should only be done by men in a mixed group. The backdrop is not a detailed one, so in most areas individual personality and culture will inform how we relate.

However, there are those who extrapolate from the evidence of the New Testament to a fully-blown theory of gender roles, attempt to ground this in Scripture and theology and claim to find corroborating evidence in biology and psychology. For example, in the widely-read volume entitled *Recovering Biblical Manhood and Womanhood* Alan Rekers writes, "In cases where the father does increase participation in child rearing, it has been suggested that the differences in the mother's and father's role in the family may become blurred as the father becomes involved in historically feminine roles. This may result in greater difficulty for children to distinguish between proper male and female roles."[21] Reker's assumption is that a universal pattern of specific activity in relation to gender identity is revealed in Scripture as "proper

---

21. Rekers, "Psychological Foundations for Rearing Masculine Boys and Feminine Girls," 307.

male and female roles." Men are the designated "bread-winners" and women are the "homemakers," despite the fact that Scripture itself does not make such a designation. Or, consider a statement like the following from Seattle pastor Mark Driscoll (commenting on 1 Tim 2:11–14): "Without blushing, Paul is simply stating that when it comes to leading in the church, women are unfit because they are more gullible and easier to deceive than men."[22] Once again, he is making a global statement about gender—and in particular women—that owes more to his own cultural assumptions about males and females than it does to Scripture itself. This is then what I would call a "strict role" description of complementarianism.

By contrast, the Sydney form of complementarianism is wary of this kind of essentialist claim and wants to uphold the profound equality of human beings expressed through the difference of roles indicated in Scripture. It would be accurate to say that most Sydney Anglicans are complementarians in the sense that they don't seek to import some view of the essential difference between men and women in the way that some (mainly American) complementarians have. The risk of this position is that it seems incomplete. It invites "thickening." After all, as a broad cultural phenomenon we can see how fascinated people are with gender and how confused they are about manhood and womanhood.[23] And yet, thickening the description of gender difference beyond the scope of Scripture may result in a coagulated mess.

But Scripture does not give us what the "strict role" complementarian wants. For example, in Ephesians 5, the submission of the wife is not complemented by the authoritative leadership or the initiative or the protective instinct of the husband. On the contrary, if the wives are to submit, then husbands are to "love your wives, just as Christ loved the church" (Eph 5:25). The mistake made in moving from complementarianism to "strict role" complementarianism is to scour Scripture for references to men and women and make them somehow universal prescriptions for patterns of gender behaviors. Often what is adduced is a very culturally conservative version of gender understood

---

22. Driscoll, *Church Leadership*, 43.

23. I note, for example, that the *Sydney Morning Herald* website hosts two blogs, "Ask Sam" and "All Men are Liars," which are specifically designed as a woman's and man's perspective on relationship issues and social mores. The presence of a difference of outlook between the genders is a given.

in "essentialist" terms.²⁴ For example, the directions that Paul gives to wives and younger women in Titus 2:5 that they are to be "busy at home" is taken not as a teaching about the situation that most younger women would have found themselves in at the time, but as somehow reflecting woman's proper and divinely prescribed station—at home looking after children.²⁵ Never mind that women like the businesswoman Lydia (Acts 16:14–15) and Chloe (1 Cor 11:1) seem to have been household heads or that the "wife of noble character" in Proverbs 31 is active in business.

Like political order, gender is a very human, culturally interpreted, and negotiated realization of the created nature of our sexed bodies. This is not, in New Testament terms, some sort of complete gender relativism. Scripture takes very seriously the human arrangement of political and social authority but also shows how these are ultimately subject to divine rule. In 1 Peter 2:13, Peter enjoins Christians to honor and submit to all "human institutions." That is: the political ordering of society is contingent and historical, a realization of delegated human authority. However, this contingence is providential (Rom 13). Unlike the modernist, who sees this historical contingence as an impetus for active subversion, the Christian submits to human orders—and "loyally resists," offering the gospel. It is the gospel that transforms and subverts, not the human will. Thus in 1 Corinthians 11 we find Paul upholding social conventions (to do with hairstyles) but with a transformed meaning (i.e., the radical mutual dependence and constitution of the genders). The cultural development of gender is not absolute, but it is not irrelevant or unauthorized. Neither is it merely arbitrary.²⁶

The New Testament does a couple of other things that unsettle a "strict role" complementarian reading of gender. First of all, it celebrates singleness as a praiseworthy and even preferable calling for some Christians (1 Cor 7). Not only was Jesus single (though he is of course symbolically married to the church), but Paul at the time of writing 1 Corinthians at least was advocating it without lapsing into an

---

24. See, for example, many of the essays in Wayne A. Grudem and John Piper, *Recovering Biblical Manhood and Womanhood: A Response to Evangelical Feminism*.

25. See Rekers, "Psychological Foundations for Rearing Masculine Boys and Feminine Girls," 310.

26. "The sexed body is the root of gender differences that are themselves always socially interpreted, negotiated and re-negotiated" (Volf, *Exclusion and Embrace*, 149).

anti-marriage asceticism. The single person is of course still gendered, but they are not expressing their gender in the socially conventional way. A single woman is not subject to a husband and yet functions as full member of the household of God without in some way being a deficient woman. On the contrary, her singleness is to be honored. The single person is a sign that the gospel of the risen and returning Christ has relativized the "natural" order of things without overturning it.

Second, the New Testament asks men to imagine themselves in the "feminine" position as members of the bride—of submitting to and responding to the loving sacrifice of Christ, the head of the church (Eph 5:22f). This is the analogy from which they are to learn, if they are husbands, to love their wives. Indeed, unless they can grasp what it is to be on the receiving end of the love of Christ and to submit to his headship, they cannot learn what it is to exercise headship. The seventeenth-century English poet John Donne rather shockingly expressed this gender reversal of faith in his poem "Batter My Heart, Three Person'd God" when, in his final line, he exclaims that he will never be "chaste, unless you ravish me."[27]

Strict role complementarianism asks for Scripture to prescribe what Christians as redeemed men and women are called on to discern in the middle of history, and so it indulges itself in poor reading of the Bible. It posits a false dichotomy between the universal and the cultural when the truth is that Scripture speaks the universal in and through the cultural. It is not an accident that, over the passage of time, those societies that have been more influenced by the Christian gospel have tended to embrace a much more egalitarian and companionate version of marriage. This is because the truth at the heart of the gospel that marriage is meant to enact is of power and authority exercised and received in loving sacrificial service for the good of the other. The notion of complementarity is not thereby overthrown. But it does mean that submission and headship will look remarkably different as the power differential between husbands and wives changes—as in fact it does. Amongst complementarian Christians that I know, marriages are remarkably egalitarian. This isn't because people haven't got the courage

---

27. It is worthy of note that the language of "submission" in the New Testament does not apply merely or even mainly to women. "Submission" is something that characterises all discipleship for both genders (see James 4:7; Eph 5:21).

of their convictions: it is because the gospel of Christ by the power of the Spirit has done its work!

Strict role complementarians have also developed the habit of dismissing "feminism" as an entirely corrupt and even deviant social movement that has caused nothing but harm. This is both simplistic and unfortunate. There were great social ills that the feminist movement challenged and overturned. The lot of women in the twenty-first century West is considerably better in many regards than it was in their great-grandmother's era and even in their grandmother's. That is not to say there aren't many, many things to critique about feminism—something that even feminists themselves would acknowledge. Nor should it be the case, as it is with many theological descriptions of feminism, that it is baptized as a movement of the Holy Spirit in history. But "feminism" is not a monolithic movement. It has many streams and tributaries. It has in many places become the norm, but continues to critique the norm. There are many issues in which evangelical Christians and some feminists will in fact be cobelligerents.[28]

A properly construed complementarianism invites men and women to receive and realize their given differentiation in the midst of actual relationships with the people in front of them; and it is also a refusal to make certain culturally-bound patterns of gender normative when there is no scriptural warrant for doing so.

Conclusion: Is It Possible for Authority to Be Other-Centered?

At the 2006 synod, Chris Albany's attempt to restart the debate on women's ordination was summarily dismissed by a large majority. Because of their stance on the ordination of women, Sydney Anglicans have come under enormous pressure from within the wider church and from the society. But after three decades of debate it has to be said that Sydney looks less like changing its mind on this than previously—at least in terms of how things work in the political process of synod. What remains, therefore, is for Sydney Anglicans to work out the full implications of their position for their common life and shared mission. There are a number of areas for careful thought.

28. Campaigning against domestic violence against women and against pornography are two examples that spring to mind.

First, at a deeper level the debate is about the nature of authority, freedom, and obedience. The gospel of Jesus Christ offers neither a recipe for anarchy nor a prescription for tyranny. It is a radical renovation of the human idea of leadership, but it is not its erasure. Christ is the head, not just because of, but precisely in, his loving sacrifice to the point of death (see Phil 2:5–11). This is authority exercised in the costly giving of the self, not in an appeal to coercion. For women to submit to such an upside-down vision of authority does not mean demeaning themselves or their innate capacity but simply letting men put themselves last. However, it is very easy for those holding the complementarian position to fall back into language that sounds as if it is promoting a coercive model of male leadership. Given the historical baggage that attaches to this issue, it is not at all surprising. In what sense, then, is discussion of this issue going to show that Christ-shaped authority is categorically different, and not an excuse for tyrannical power? Given the tendency of men to be seduced by power, how are they to be held accountable as husbands and church leaders for their use of it? The Sydney Anglican position is not naive, but it is one held by faith: faith in the possibility of other-centered power, faith that the gospel can so transform men that they wield their authority for the good of women, at radical cost to themselves.

Second, if Sydney wishes to express a biblically-derived gender differentiation in its leadership, it needs also to ask where plain old sexism exists and work doubly hard to overcome it. There needs to be not a hint of it. Sydney Anglicans have to work hard to overcome the cynicism of those who oppose them and demonstrate that they really do believe in the fundamental equality of worth of the genders. This might mean taking the lead in advocating against violence against women, for instance, as a matter of priority. It means finding opportunities to advance the liberty and opportunities of women in the church and in the community.

Third, Sydney needs to develop its understanding of ministry and marriage as a partnership between men and women. Though many women offer the ministry and study at Moore College, often these women are employed in churches to do "women's ministry" as if it were a secret female business and not employed on the basis that they are partners in the whole ministry. The current restrictions against women teaching from the front in many parishes are not always matched by a creative use of their gifts elsewhere. The practice of prophesying discussed in 1 Corinthians 11 shows that Paul did expect women to speak in the church gathering in some capacity—and yet this practice is honored more often in the breach. If the genders really are complementary, then they ought not to be segregated in the shared task of honoring Christ.

ten

The Great Cause? The Push for Lay Administration at the Lord's Supper

The Lord's Supper in Non-Ordained Hands?

Around the Anglican Communion, the Sydney diocese has become known—has become notorious indeed—for its advocacy of lay and diaconal administration at the Lord's Supper. Although it makes good sense to most Sydney Anglicans as an appropriate reform of church order in the light of Scripture and according to the needs of mission, lay presidency (the preferred local term is "administration") is seen as further evidence of the sheer deliberate contrariness of Sydney's Anglicans. The more cynical critics read the push for lay administration as an attempt to undercut women's ordination and as counterclaim against the advances made by progressives and Anglo-Catholics.

In fact, advocacy for lay administration is at one level entirely consistent with the Reformation convictions of the Sydney diocese. It can hardly be seen as merely a response to progressivist victories. It has been offered as a proposal for more than thirty-five years, which preempts many of the current debates within Anglicanism. The Sydney approach has been consultative and cautious. Advocates of women's ordination did not wait for legal and synodical approval but openly flouted the agreed laws of the church in 1992 by going ahead. Archbishop Peter Carnley of Perth and Bishop Owen Dowling of Canberra-Goulburn showed scant regard for the ecclesial order they in other circumstances would vehemently uphold. This has not occurred in Sydney with lay administration.

Priestly administration at the Lord's Supper is not a gospel issue but very much a second-order one on which there ought to be freedom. That freedom, however, is a gift to use in the cause of the gospel. Is it the case that there is far more for Sydney to lose in opportunities for leadership within national and global Anglicanism than there is to be gained by pressing ahead? Though there is no "theological objection" to lay administration—on the basis that Scripture is silent on the matter—the reality is far more complex. Scripture is *not* silent about church order, and this makes it very much a theological issue for which there may well be significant theological objections. The advocacy of lay administration has proceeded on the basis of certain assumptions about what is being communicated in our current practice from an evangelical perspective both from a pastoral and a missional point of view. The first of these is that celebration of the Holy Communion by the ordained clergyman must surely convey that the ministry involved is sacerdotal. It is worth asking whether this assumption is warranted.

The underlying problem is, in fact, more serious and has to do with the Lord's Supper itself. What the proposal for, and the response to, lay administration reveals is that there are two (at least!) very different and incompatible understandings of the Lord's Supper within Anglican churches today.

The Story of Lay Presidency

For those born since 1970, it is a surprise to learn that lay involvement in the ministries of the church has been a development really only since the 1960s. Lay assistance at the Holy Communion was only permitted in Sydney in 1969, even though this practice has been widespread elsewhere in the Communion and in the Anglican Church of Australia prior to this. It is interesting to note the concern for due legal process that is part of the Sydney mentality at work here. In those days of course the evangelical adherence to prayer-book Anglicanism was far stricter, as a defense against Anglo-Catholic innovations. However, the spirit of the times was a leveling spirit. Egalitarianism in ministry seemed to be quite congenial with the evangelical emphasis on the priesthood of all believers. In the 1970s, successive ordinances of Sydney synod authorized lay involvement in all kinds of ministries usually reserved for the clergy—including lay preaching.

In 1977, the Sydney synod requested a local discussion on the matter of lay involvement in the ministries of word and sacrament. This went forward despite the general synod of the national church declaring itself against the idea of lay administration. The Diocesan Doctrine Commission was requested by the 1981 synod to bring them report, which they took two years to complete. By early 1984 they had conclude that there was no impediment, historically or theologically, to lay administration.[1] In 1985, the later archbishop of Sydney, Harry Goodhew, successfully moved that the synod "endorses the principle of lay presidency and requests the Standing Committee to investigate ways the possible legal and other difficulties in enacting this principle could be overcome." Further committee work on the legal and theological issues further established that there was in their opinion no obstacle to lay administration. Archbishop Donald Robinson, however, indicated that he would not endorse any move to establish lay presidency by the Sydney synod. Once Harry Goodhew became archbishop, he began to feel some of the same misgivings. With an awareness of the sensitivity of the issue in other parts of the country and indeed within global Anglicanism, Goodhew lost his enthusiasm for lay presidency and declared this in his synod address in 1993.

Consultation with other parts of the Anglican church in Australia has been extensive. In 1995, the Sydney synod asked the appellate tribunal—a "court" of appeal for the national church consisting of theologians and lawyers—to give its opinion on the question of lay presidency. This question was in fact withdrawn when the primate referred his own questions on the matter to the tribunal:

> 1. Is it consistent with the Constitution of the Anglican Church of Australia to permit or authorize, or otherwise make provision for
>
>> a. Deacons to preside at, administer or celebrate the Holy Communion; or
>> b. Lay persons to preside at, administer or celebrate the Holy Communion?
>
> 2. If the whole or any part of the answer to Question 1 is YES, is it consistent with the Constitution of the Anglican Church of

---

1. Bolt, Thompson, and Tong, *The Lord's Supper in Human Hands*, 42.

The Great Cause? The Push for Lay Administration at the Lord's Supper

Australia for a diocesan Synod, otherwise than under and in accordance with a Canon of General Synod, to permit, authorize, or make provision as mentioned in Question 1?

The appellate tribunal took more than two years to give its opinion, which effectively stalled the progress of the issue within the Sydney synod. In the end they answered "Yes" to 1a, "Yes" to 1b, but a definite "No" to 2. That is to say, the tribunal decided that lay and diaconal presidency was certainly permissible and consistent, but that it could only happen with the approval of the national church—a diocese could not act alone.[2] This proved crucial—for when the Sydney synod finally gave the green light to a five-year trial of lay presidency in 1999, Archbishop Goodhew withheld his assent. He noted that the Lambeth conference 1998 had called on bishops not to act unilaterally with regard to the affirmation of homosexual practice; that he had supported this call; and that it would now look hypocritical to act unilaterally on this matter when something far more significance was at stake.

Since 2000, the cause for lay administration has somewhat slowed. In one sense, the synod vote of 1999—which had decisively affirmed it—was as far as a synod could go. The matter was brought before the general synod of 2004 and given extensive debate but rejected. It became clear that the preferred option for "emergency" situations in most other dioceses was "local ordinations," in which a person was ordained but only to a single parish. How this made theological sense when lay presidency was to be rejected was unclear.

What this short summary of the history shows is that Sydney's proponents of lay administration have been cautious and consultative over a long period of time. They have put forward their case carefully and openly. Though gossip and anecdote circulates about Sydney churches that practice lay administration, the reality is that there has not been a cavalier attitude to church order at all on this issue. While there may be some isolated counterexamples, parishes have not pressed ahead regardless—in contrast to progressivist actions over women's ordination and the consecration of actively homosexual bishops. As Tom Frame has written in his book *Anglicans in Australia*, the way Sydney has conducted this debate shows "a capacity for generosity of spirit and a genuine regard for the divergent opinions of others within

2. Once again, the tension between the more federalist view of the Australian Anglican Church and its dioceses (held by Sydney) and the centralist model surfaces.

147

the Australian Church and the Anglican Communion."[3] He goes one to say: "the diocese has shown genuine regard for prevailing sentiment within the Anglican Communion by recognizing and respecting the limits of diversity that the Communion would appear ready to tolerate. Such regard, however, has been noticeably absent in other parts of the Communion in relation to another controversial issue, a matter on which the Bible is far from silent."[4]

Why Lay Presidency?

In one sense the case for lay administration (the preferred terminology) is very simple—so simple indeed that the proponents of the change have not really felt the need to produce lengthy monographs in its defense. It is an argument from silence. Scripture, which is authoritative for Anglicans, does not mention who should preside at Holy Communion and lays down no directive on this matter. To prohibit administration of the Lord's Supper by non-ordained persons makes a rule where Scripture has no rule. Even a writer like Nicholas H. Taylor, whose stated purpose it is to defend priest-only celebration, has to concede that the evidence of the New Testament—and even what can be reconstructed around the New Testament—says little to support his view.[5]

Scripture seems to allow liberty in this matter. But proponents wish to make a strong case *for* lay administration on the grounds that the current restrictive practice is a distortion of the gospel itself.[6] The historical context has changed since the *Book of Common Prayer* and the *Ordinal* were formulated, especially in the area of lay ministry. Laypeople are permitted and even encouraged to preach, to read the Scriptures, to pray and to assist at the Lord's Supper. Why has this one last activity been withheld? It seems to be inconsistent, and it communicates a theology of the Eucharist that evangelicals would not wish to uphold. It conveys the impression that there is a special power in the ordination to pray the prayer of consecration. It indicates that there is a higher priority in this activity than in preaching the word of God. It suggests that the validity of the Lord's Supper is constituted by the one

3. Frame, *Anglicans in Australia*, 182.
4. Ibid., 188.
5. Taylor, *Lay Presidency at the Eucharist*, 62.
6. Bolt, Thompson, and Tong, *The Lord's Supper in Human Hands*, 7.

who administers it and that ordination has more to do with the sacrament than the ministry of the word. Though the prohibition against a layperson administering the Lord's Supper was at first of godly intent, it now reflects an inconsistent and incoherent theology of word and sacrament.

That is to say: evangelical Anglicans have never accepted the Anglo-Catholic interpretation of the significance of the Holy Communion, in which the elements become themselves a means of grace and which requires a quasi-Roman Catholic understanding of the nature of ordination as a priestly ministry. In fact, they hold that it adds to the gospel of grace. For them, the only "means of grace" is the word of God. As far as the sacraments are effective it is because they are related to and derived from the word of God. For a long time the ambiguity of the *BCP* and the English live-and-let-live attitude have allowed multiple understandings of the Supper to coexist within the same church order. Yet the context has changed markedly with the great involvement of laypeople in public ministry, introducing an imbalance into the understanding of ordained ministry and its nature. Liturgical revisions since the 1970s across the Anglican Communion have frequently made more explicitly Catholic the services of the Lord's Supper. Advocating lay administration is a way of asserting the credibility of the evangelical view of the ministry and the sacraments.

The formularies of the Church of England explicitly restrict the administration of the Lord's Supper to the priest or presbyter. However, a move to lay administration is arguably consistent with the Reformation principles to which the Church of England also subscribed. Given contemporary church practices regarding lay involvement in ministry, the reserving of one particular act to the ordained person present seems curious and counter to the Reformation principle of the "priesthood of all believers." Though administration was restricted in the Anglican formularies, it was not on account of a theology of ordination that held that the priest was standing between God and the people. On the contrary, it was out of concern for good order in the Church in a period when superstitions abounded. As with preaching, the restriction of the celebration of the Lord's Supper to the priest made it possible to hold someone accountable for its practice.

Furthermore, the formularies of Anglicanism consistently bind word and sacrament, with the ministry of the word taking priority over the sacrament. The "Theological Statement of the English House of Bishops" (1997) on the matter of lay presidency remarks that behind the wording of the *Book of Common Prayer* lay

> . . . a conviction to be found in all the mainline reformers about the intimate connection between word and sacrament. Ministers are ordained to the ministry of the word and sacrament, and both convey the evangelical promises of grace. The sacraments must not be allowed to take on a life of their own for they are subordinate to the proclamation and reception of the word. The case which the mainstream reformers made for restricting the Ministry of the Sacrament to appointed ministers rests ultimately on their understanding of the indissolubility of words and sacrament, and the dependence of the latter on the former. The Ministry of the Word is made available and applied to the life of the Church only through authorized ordained ministers—so it should be with the sacraments (para 4.35).

The theological statement itself decides strongly against lay presidency. It has to acknowledge, however, that the founding documents of Anglicanism inextricably link word and sacrament. Anything which would symbolically break that link would, one would think, have been grounds for revision of church order. Given that no one of any churchmanship is opposed to the development of lay preaching as a normal practice since the 1960s, it would seem that the link described in the "Theological Statement" has already been cracked. If the lay preacher can preach under the delegated authority of the ordained minister, why can she not administer the Lord's Supper under that same delegated authority?

There is great deal of what must only be called rank hypocrisy in some of the opposition to lay administration. Innovations such as "extended Communion" or "reserved sacrament"—by which the elements are consecrated in one place and carried by a deacon or layperson to another place, often a hospital bedside or a distant branch church—reflect a view of the Eucharist that evangelical Anglicans would reject as inconsistent with the Anglican formularies. It conveys the impression that the elements themselves have actually *changed* in some way, such as that they are now sacred objects. In article 25 "Of the Sacraments" it says "The Sacraments were not ordained of Christ to be gazed upon, or to be carried about, but that we should duly use them." Article 27, "Of the Lord's Supper," goes on to explicitly deny the Roman Catholic teaching on transubstantiation and repeats the prohibition on carrying the elements about: "Transubstantiation (or the change of the substance of Bread and Wine) in the Supper of the Lord, cannot be proved by holy Writ; but is repugnant to the plain words of Scripture, overthroweth the nature of a Sacrament, and hath given occasion to many superstitions. . . . The Sacrament of the Lord's Supper was not by Christ's ordinance reserved, carried about, lifted up, or worshiped."

It would be specious to argue (as John Henry Newman did in his *Tracts for the Times*) that some other view of the metaphysics of the change in the elements in the Communion service is envisaged here. The emphasis in the Supper according to the *Articles* is not on the change in the elements, but the change in the believer, who "feeds in your heart by faith with thanksgiving." The *Book of Common Prayer* insists that, after the Communion service, "the Priest and such other of the Communicants as he shall then call unto him, shall immediately after the Blessing, reverently eat and drink the same." The act of consuming the leftover elements is an explicit denial of the suggestion that the elements have in some way become metaphysically changed in the service of Communion. To allow extended Communions would be to contravene this principle established in the formularies themselves.

The case for permissible change is bolstered by article 34, "It is not necessary that Traditions and Ceremonies be in all places one, and utterly like; for at all times they have been divers, and may be changed according to the diversities of countries, times, and men's manners, so that nothing be ordained against God's Word. . . . Every particular or national Church hath authority to ordain, change, and abolish, ceremonies or rites of the Church ordained only by man's authority, so that all things be done to edifying."

That is to say, the *Articles* envisage a time when customs will need to change to reflect new contexts in the light of Scripture. Though the Lord's Supper is not a rite "ordained only by man's authority," the restriction of the act of presiding at the meal to the ordained priest certainly is. A change in circumstances—such as the acceptance of lay ministries in other aspects of church life—at least seems to provide a warrant for a change in practices.

Nicholas H. Taylor's Lay Presidency at the Eucharist

Despite these arguments, opposition to Sydney's proposal has been extremely strong from other parts of the Anglican world—even from churches who are allied with Sydney in the GAFCON movement. This proposal seems to be a step too far for many Anglicans, even evangelical ones.

An Anglican priest working in South Africa, Nicholas H. Taylor has written a substantial and sophisticated response to the proposal for lay presidency titled *Lay Presidency at the Eucharist? An Anglican Approach*. It has to be said that the depth and seriousness of Taylor's book rather outweigh the short polemical pieces and committee papers that have been offered by those advocating lay administration. He offers an extensive and nuanced discussion of the nature of authority in Anglicanism and on the whole gives a careful exposition of the case for lay administration before countering it with his own.

Two features of his argument mar it, however. The first is that he attempts to say what "Anglican" is, but can only do so by making his own, more Catholic interpretation of the Lord's Supper paradigmatic for all Anglican practice. The problem comes when you romanticize the Anglican compromise as a wonderful synthesis, instead of acknowledging that the ambiguity in the formularies made possible, within the same ecclesiastical structure, the presence of two mutually exclusive views of the Eucharist, and that the fragility of this compromise meant that it resolved nothing and was always going to fall apart at some point. Taylor is unable to acknowledge the legitimate and continuous presence of the alternative reading of the sacraments in the Anglican tradition, and fails to argue against it on its own terms. What he discovers is only that the Anglican evangelical view of the sacraments is not the same as the Anglo-Catholic one. This is not particularly newsworthy.

Second, though Taylor is for the most part a model of scholarly dispassion, when he comes to engaging with the diocese of Sydney he is unable to contain himself and slips into polemic. He calls Sydney "an ultra-Protestant fringe of Anglicanism" whose "interpretations of the Bible and the Book of Common Prayer may alike be tendentious, and account of the historically somewhat liminal place this diocese has taken in the Anglican Communion, and even in the Anglican Church

The Great Cause? The Push for Lay Administration at the Lord's Supper

of Australia."[7] The word "liminal"—a word Taylor repeats—is the strange one here. Does he mean by it "barely perceptible" or "a transitory state?"[8] In any case, it is clear that Taylor wants to portray these, the most serious advocates for the position he wants to counter, as extremists and eccentrics barely worth taking seriously. He adds to this impression by pointing out to his readers the connection that Sydney diocese has maintained over a number of decades with "the schismatic ecclesial group known as the Church of England in South Africa, which maintained close ties with the apartheid regime."[9] This is a largely irrelevant statement designed only to taint Sydney Anglicans with racism in the mind of his readers and so utterly prejudice the outcome of his discussion. The complex history of the "other" Anglicans in South Africa is by no means without its regretful aspects (for which its bishop, Frank Retief, made a public declaration of apology and repentance in the 1990s[10]), yet the phrase "close ties" would be more than an exaggeration.[11] The argument for Sydney's "liminality" means that he overlooks the long and vigorous history of evangelicals within the Church of England in almost every place that the Church of England has gone.

Taylor points out that while in many instances the argument for lay administration is driven by the practical problem of the lack of ordained clergy—most often in rural districts—in Sydney there is no such shortage compared to other dioceses. This observation is correct, although there are a greater number of people in congregations in Sydney Anglican churches, too. It is certainly difficult for a complete outsider to the diocese in question to offer his view on the practical needs of the ministry. He does not take into account the way in which the development of new congregations has put pressure on the current system of ordination. Nevertheless, he is correct to understand Sydney's push for lay administration as theologically driven and not just pragmatic.

Taylor takes Archbishop Peter Jensen to task for depending heavily on Cranmer's views as normative for Anglicanism in his argument for

---

7. Taylor, *Lay Presidency at the Eucharist*, 186.
8. Definitions found at http://www.merriam-webster.com/dictionary/liminal.
9. Taylor, *Lay Presidency at the Eucharist*, 186.
10. See chapter 8.
11. For a more detailed account of the history of CESA, see http://cesa.org.za/history.html.

lay administration.[12] This would be to overstate the claims that Jensen makes for Cranmer in his short piece on the subject. And yet, it would seem to strange to argue that, as the primary author of the Anglican formularies, Cranmer's views are of very limited importance to the discussion. Taylor is right to point to the fact that Cranmer argues strongly for administration of the sacrament only by those duly authorized by lawful authority—but then, this is not really in dispute.

Taylor then tries to mount a strange argument that the argument for lay presidency is actually designed to uphold hierarchical and patriarchal patterns within the diocese of Sydney: "It is not envisaged that delegation to lay people of functions such as preaching and administering holy communion in Sunday worship would involve any participation in the pastoral oversight exercised by the Archbishop and clergy of the diocese of Sydney. Power would remain vested in an exclusive male cadre, formed principally and definitively at Moore Theological College in the very particular and narrow theological tradition which Sydney represents."[13]

The issue of lay presidency, he argues, must be linked to Sydney's resistance to women's ordination. If laypeople—females among them—can be admitted to the business administering Communion as well as Communion, then what is it that not ordaining them excludes them from? Taylor deduces that it must be all about conserving the power of the clique, or the "cadre," as he calls it. What ordination represents, in Taylor's reading of the Sydney mentality, is not preaching or presiding, but power. This is a kind of postmodern power-critique of the predictable kind, but it relies on speculation about the motives of others to which Taylor is certainly not privy. With respect, how is Taylor able to see what it is really about from his study on the other side of the Indian Ocean?

In fact, push for lay administration in Sydney began quite separately to and at around about the same time as the call of women's ordination began in the wider Anglican Communion. Certainly, the proponents of lay administration have wanted to show that their understanding of ordination was not a specifically sacramental one and that their objection to women's ordination was not on the basis of the Anglo-Catholic reasoning about sacerdotal ministry. If anything,

12. Jensen, "Theological Reflection on Lay Administration."
13. Taylor, *Lay Presidency at the Eucharist*, 195.

however, lay administration would open up leadership opportunities for laymen and women and for female deacons in Sydney, which is a diocese with a long history of active lay leadership by both genders and which employs more women in ministry than any other. Taylor's comments about the "particular and narrow theological tradition" represented by Sydney reveal only that he overlooks the ongoing presence of evangelicals within Anglicanism around the globe. If it is only in Sydney that they have been able to influence an entire diocese in the way they have, it is because of the political hegemony of the liberal Catholic party elsewhere. Most dioceses in the world would represent a "very particular and narrow theological tradition"—namely, the liberal Catholic one—under whose powerful rule it is oftentimes very difficult for evangelicals to live.

Taylor makes a great deal of an almost throwaway comment by Archbishop Peter Jensen. In advocating for liturgical change, Jensen described the current forms of liturgy as "almost irrelevant" in the context of contemporary mission. By this he did not mean, as Taylor takes him to mean, that the gathering together of the people of God around the word and sacrament was irrelevant—only that the forms in which we have continued to practice our meeting have become inaccessible and impenetrable to the secularized world. Yet Taylor riffs on this phrase, claiming that, "As a theology of the laity, it denigrates the people of God to whom the 'almost irrelevant' ministry of word and sacrament is entrusted, while clergy are engaged in the ministry which really matters."[14]

This is an unfortunate misreading, and it is certainly not the intention of those who argue for lay administration. What Taylor ignores is the vigorous support for lay administration from laypeople themselves within the diocese of Sydney. Far from being a plot by the men at head office to shore up their own power, the envisaged change is meant to complete the "lay revolution" begun in the late 1960s by admitting laypeople to the ministry of the table as well as the ministry of the pulpit.

Taylor's book is an otherwise very accomplished and judicious work, mostly carried out with appropriate scholarly reserve. At the end of his extended review of the subject, he argues that the issue of who presides at the Lord's Supper is a second-order issue, and that it is permissible in certain emergency situations. From Taylor's point of view, the most suitable solution to the shortage of clergy is the ordination of

14. Ibid.

local Christian leadership as "the most satisfactory alternative to authorized lay presidency at the Eucharist."[15] I fail to see what the difference between lay administration and local ordination is, especially if you do not share a more Catholic view of ordination. It is nowhere envisaged that lay administration would mean unauthorized administration—there would have to be a system of due authorization of lay ministers, just as there is for lay preachers. And the authorization would hold for the services in the local parish and not elsewhere. Is the difference between lay administration and local ordination only then a matter of what you call it? It would seem so—unless you have a quasi-mystical view of the effects of ordination. Local ordination is no less a novelty than lay administration. So why is this alternative preferable and the Sydney suggestion anathema?

Holding Back?

Sydney Anglicans have with great patience and restraint argued its case for lay administration over many years. They have marveled at the way in which this has been equated with the open endorsement of a form of immorality against which Scripture directly speaks in other Anglican churches. They have been astonished at the passionate response to this attempt to change church order when significant challenges to orthodox doctrine and ethics go unremarked. They have been surprised at the innovations contemplated in the name of equality and mission, but resisted on this particular matter. If lay administration is a second-order issue, as even Taylor will admit, then why has it elicited so much hostility?

Despite all of this, should Sydney go ahead with lay administration in the foreseeable future? I don't think that there are any *theological* objections insofar as I would (and have) happily receive the Lord's Supper in a Baptist church from a layperson and consider that the sacrament was in no way deficient—in fact, I would find it offensive were any Anglican to suggest it was in some way an incomplete celebration. However, there are still a number of issues that need addressing.

First, despite what some of its proponents claim, it is not in fact a "gospel issue." Calling it a gospel issue posits an either-or that is simply

15. Ibid., 176.

not accurate. The reason for calling it a gospel issue is that reserving the act of administration at the Supper for the ordained priest/presbyter allegedly communicates a view of the sacrament which sets it apart from the word and makes it a special means of grace in addition to the gospel in some way—along the lines of a Roman Catholic theology of the sacraments. However, there is no sense in which a Communion service run in the evangelical parishes of the diocese of Sydney could ever be confused in that way. The usual practice communicates anything but a sacerdotal view of the Supper. The ministers do not normally robe or even wear collars these days. The locally authorized liturgies specifically rule out a sacerdotal interpretation of the Communion. Who administers at the Supper becomes then a matter of church order rather than of the gospel itself.

Second, Sydney diocese has an enormous opportunity for a leadership of service within the Anglican Communion in the first decades of the twenty-first century—in countries where it is often difficult to be a Christian such as Egypt, Madagascar, and Myanmar. Anglicans in these countries may class themselves as "evangelicals" but may often just understand themselves to be "Anglican" without reference to a party. They are conservative in theological outlook and looking for help in mission. They are reluctant to accept it from the liberal wing of the church, especially from the Episcopal Church of the USA that they feel has become morally compromised since consecrating two actively homosexual bishops. They are concerned that the same spirit of private judgment and self-legislation without wider consultation is at play in Sydney. Perhaps in Sydney we may dispute their judgment on this matter and point to the arduous process of deliberation and consultation that has been undertaken. And yet cooperation with these churches is an opportunity for proclaiming Jesus.

Third, evangelicals in other parts of the Anglican Communion aren't calling for it with any enthusiasm. At present, many evangelicals look to Sydney for support and to see what might be achieved by evangelicals within an Anglican framework. That relationship would certainly be compromised by pushing ahead with lay administration. Sydney-trained clergy in other parts of the world would be given fewer opportunities and viewed with greater suspicion as a result of this change. In fact, Sydney-trained clergy serving outside Sydney have often called on Sydney to exercise restraint in this matter.

Fourth, simply as a matter of tactics, lay administration is arguably ill-advised. Currently, the North American liberals are rending the Anglican Communion apart with their innovations. They have acted precipitously and selfishly. They have severely compromised the integrity of the Anglican Communion. The Sydney diocese does not share, as a matter ecclesiological conviction, the view of the unity of the Communion that others do. However, moving forward with lay presidency offers a chance for people to compare the two kinds of innovation and to view them as equivalent. A Communion wanting to appear even-handed may expel Sydney just as it expels ECUSA. Far better to allow the crises over homosexual bishops to play itself out in the Communion and see what new state of play eventuates then to give those whose hatred of Sydney is implacable a cause to move against it.

Fifth, it is really the case that a practical necessity drives lay administration in Sydney? There are plenty of candidates for ministry, and plenty of serving presbyters—certainly compared to other dioceses. The current practice is for a monthly Communion or perhaps less. Almost every practical concern could be overcome. The current policy of only ordaining as presbyters those who are rectors is perhaps an obstacle, in that congregational leaders may frequently not be presbyters. Diaconal administration—which is currently in the process of being legalized—has made this need less urgent.

Sixth, even though in my judgment no real case of any substance has been put against lay administration, the arguments have singularly failed to convince the wider Anglican Communion even slightly, let alone others in the Australian church. Many of those not convinced would count themselves as dear friends of the Sydney diocese. Whatever one's opinion of the matter, this is precisely the opposite of the case with women's ordination, where a clear majority of the Australian church were in favor. It may seem that almost four decades is a long time to be considering a change such as this. Could Sydney really push ahead with the change without majority approval at a national level?

This may seem like a surprising conclusion given all that has come before it. However it is arguably more consistent with the Christian gospel, which enjoins us not to insist on our own rights but to consider the needs of others. For a chance of sharing with the Anglicans of Myanmar or Egypt or Chile in their call to preach the gospel, I would readily lay down my insistence on a particular change of church order. That really

The Great Cause? The Push for Lay Administration at the Lord's Supper

is a gospel issue. Though no substantial arguments have appeared to counter lay administration at a theological level, here is an opportunity to show patient endurance for the sake of others.

eleven

Church Politics and the Anglican Church League

The Necessity of Church Politics

In his book *The Chosen Ones: The Politics of Salvation in the Anglican Church* journalist Chris McGillion paints a somewhat unflattering picture of the inner workings of the diocese of Sydney over the 1993–2003 period.[1] Crafted chiefly from interviews with some of the protagonists, it is a story of maneuverings, tactics, parties, and vote-counting. Some of those interviewed seemed, like old war heroes, to relish the chance to recount the cut-and-thrust of those days—oblivious to the interviewer's distaste, which he assumes that his implied reader will share. McGillion's thesis is that the Sydney Anglicans who came to power in those years had a belief that they were "the chosen ones"—and that this justified to them the use of nakedly political means in the godly cause to which they had been called. From McGillion's point of view, politics is an ugly business even when it pursues apparently holy ends. His subjects did not seem to share this embarrassment. It is this clash of perspectives that makes the book an intriguing read.

The subject of ecclesiastical politics is frequently associated with Sydney Anglicans, not because they invented it, but because they have been remarkably good at it. The refined disdain for the political aspect of church life is a luxury afforded those to whom power naturally tends to accrue. Like all human institutions, churches need a decision-making process. As a body politic, it has bodily-political functions that need attending to. It is not an unspiritual thing to seek to manage these as

---

1. McGillion, *The Chosen Ones*.

effectively as possible, however crass it might seem to those of more sophisticated palate. Sometimes it is a messy and complicated business—a process that presents unenviable choices and imperfect solutions.

That being said, success in the process has perhaps obscured the consideration of the possibility that the process itself might be deeply flawed and could be reformed. As has been frequently pointed out, synods as they are presently constituted have far too many members to be an efficient chamber of debate and discussion and are inevitably dominated by lawyers and those of a political disposition. Sydney Anglicans have twice as many representatives in their synod than the Australian people do in their parliament! Inevitably, with such an unwieldy process the distribution of power and the mutual accountability that a democratic process is meant to ensure becomes concentrated in the hands of smaller committees. And it almost *requires* the development of the group whose history is inextricably linked to the history of the Sydney diocese: the Anglican Church League.

The Rise of the Anglican Church League

The Australian form of Anglicanism has a long history of embracing synodical government. Without the deeply embedded alliance with the Crown and the Parliament to help it, as was the case in England, the Australian church had to find a way to order its own affairs. In fact, as Tom Frame writes, "The Australian Church led the Anglican Communion in its embrace of synodical government."[2] The word "synod" emerges from a Greek word *sunodos*, which means "assembly" or "meeting." There being no prescribed method of decision-making for churches in the New Testament, synods have varied enormously in size, task, and process over the two millennia of church history. In the Church of England, synods had a rather peripheral role given that the church was governed by royal supremacy via parliament and the convocation of bishops. The colonials, for their part, wanted an arrangement which ensured the more direct involvement of the laity in parallel with the secular parliaments. This meant that synods have largely adopted the parliamentary processes and legal mechanisms of the British parliament. From 1872 there was a national, "General" synod and corresponding diocesan

2. Frame, *A House Divided?*, 114.

synods. Given the great distances involved in most Australian diocese, the diocesan synod became in many places the most significant opportunity for clergy and laity to share fellowship.

Sydney's synod was first convened in 1866 by Bishop Barker (1808–1882). The sessions were lengthy and demanded a high level of competence from its participants. Whereas before the bishop relied somewhat informally on carefully chosen lay and clerical advisors in order to make decisions, now this gathering of high-powered laity and clergy had its own decision making function. As the historians of the Sydney diocese, Judd and Cable write, "by the end of Barker's episcopate, synod had emerged in an effective form as the focus of the diocese."[3]

In these early years the synod needed to set the affairs of the diocese in order. The parliamentarians, lawyers, and landowners that held positions on synod ensured that proper standing orders were introduced, the financial arrangements of the diocese established, and a standing committee appointed. For clergy, the rise of the synod meant that they were no longer vulnerable to the whims of their bishop. There was now a system of nominations and a degree of professional security. Theological and social issues did not arise and were not debated—there was not initially a sense that there were mutually incompatible theological visions that would need to assert themselves in this forum.

Up until the 1890s, it was still however the case that the synod tended to see itself as chiefly supportive of the bishop in his management of the diocese. In 1897, the standing committee was granted authority to act "without prior reference to the full synod."[4] The rate of legislation increased and indicated that the exclusive power of the bishop over his diocese was certainly at an end.

The emergence of party groupings in the synod can be dated to this period. Becoming a busier legislative chamber inevitably led to divisions just because of the adversarial nature of the process, with winners and losers. In 1886 the Church of England Association, a lay organization, was formed. The association's stated aim was to prevent the advance of ritualism in the church; and it proved to be successful in achieving this end. Throughout the 1890s other political groupings emerged representing the Anglo-Catholics, High Churchmen, and

3. Judd and Cable, *Sydney Anglicans*, 92.
4. Ibid., 142.

others. It was the Protestant Church of England Union, an evangelical alliance, which emerged as the strongest group in the diocese by the turn of the century. The Union was determined to stop Anglo-Catholic practices and pressured the archbishop to act on their behalf against the introduction of eucharistic vestments.

Once Archbishop Wright had made a strong stand against the introduction of such vestments in Sydney, the PCEU found that the wind was taken out of its sails somewhat. A new evangelical party, the Anglican Church League, emerged in 1909 as a party of broad evangelical consensus. The founder of the league, Canon Francis Bertie Boyce (1844–1931), was determined that evangelicals would not merely present a reactionary, defensive, and increasingly isolated place in the Church. The League would rather pursue a constructive and reasonable evangelical policy, finding as it did so as much common ground between evangelicals as it could. It would fight strongly for the principles of the Reformation but it intended to do so from a position of centrist strength and not from the fringe. In the words of Judd and Cable, "they were not about to be isolated as a lunatic fringe; they were determined to be a party of comprehension, not narrowly exclusive."[5]

From this broad base, the ACL was able to achieve considerable political success in the Sydney synod. It did this because its relatively small actual membership remained united and because it was brilliantly directed by an even smaller executive group. It also succeeded because it was led by clergymen who had the time and inclination to attend to church affairs. In addition, the League sponsored lectures and events on evangelical themes, and it further revived the evangelical newspaper the *Church Record*.

In the view of historians Judd and Cable the secret to the ACL's success was its pre-selection of candidates for diocesan elections—caucusing, in other words. This was not a novelty in church affairs—indeed caucusing is of ancient provenance. What was new was that evangelicals were doing the caucusing. And it was astutely done. The League's policy was to pre-select not only strong evangelicals but also to elect a proportion of High Churchmen to various diocesan positions. This somewhat disarmed the High Church opposition, who were given a share of the power but only on the terms set for them by the League. By the mid-1920s, the ACL had achieved dominance in electoral terms.

5. Ibid., 167.

The proportional representation policy helped to quieten dissent and discontent.

By the mid-1930s, however, the broad evangelical consensus under which the League had first gathered its membership had broken. At the election of Howard Mowll (1890–1958) to the see of Sydney in April 1933, the conservative evangelicals asserted themselves over against the liberal evangelicals led by the dean, A. E. Talbot (1877–1936) and the principal of Moore College, D. J. Davies (1879–1935). Talbot and Davies were also the president and a vice president of the ACL at the time. These two men now resigned from the League and set up a new, more liberal, grouping, the Anglican Fellowship. This was a real challenge to the conservative evangelicals, who now felt that something of theological importance was at stake. The liberal evangelicals were more vague about the authority of Scripture and less definite that the atoning blood of Jesus Christ was central to the gospel. The business of the synod was not merely now a matter of keeping the diocese operating smoothly. With the increasingly emergence and influence of a more liberal evangelicalism, it was now a contest about the theological commitments that would mark the Church of England in Sydney.

For the first time, the ACL not only nominated its own candidates in synod elections, it issued a how-to-vote ticket. This was an immediately successful strategy and continued to be so throughout the 1930s, such that Anglican Fellowship completely died away. Upon the death of Principal Davies in 1935, Archbishop Mowll appointed the singularly remarkable Irishman T. C. Hammond—arguably the greatest intellect in the conservative evangelical world—to the principalship of Moore College. Along with these two men, the League now pursued the goal of securing the specifically conservative evangelical character of the diocese. By the mid-1950s, it could be safely said that it was a strategy that had largely succeeded.

The League and the Archbishops

Even so, the one uncertain factor for the League has always turned out to be the figure of the archbishop of Sydney. The ACL has not always played their game astutely at archiepiscopal elections, and more often than not the compromise candidate has been the one who has eventually succeeded. Furthermore, the ACL is dominated by leading clergy, who tend to have an innate mistrust of bishops—even the ones they have helped to elect. The reality is that the archbishop of Sydney sits at the hub of an enormous and relatively well-resourced see; and so it is not surprising that archbishops of Sydney tend to develop their own views on things.

In between 1932 and 2001, the ACL has had very mixed success in archiepiscopal elections. Archbishop Mowll was the high-water mark of conservative evangelicalism as far as the ACL was concerned. He was conservative evangelical to the bootstraps, uncompromising and charismatic in style, and concerned about evangelism and expansion. When Mowll died in 1958, it was not obvious who would replace him. The League was unable to agree on a single candidate and so their support was split among the locals: Bishops Hilliard, Kerle, and Loane. The alternative candidate was the bishop of Barking in the diocese of Chelmsford, UK—Hugh Gough (1905-1997). Gough had impeccable evangelical credentials, but had a more comprehensive outlook than the others, and so garnered all of the non-evangelical votes. An Englishman of somewhat autocratic bearing in an age when Australia was beginning to assert itself, it was not surprising that Gough's tenure was onerous. He resigned a full ten years before his due, in 1966.

The elections of Archbishops Loane (1966) and Robinson (1982) were by all accounts not marked by controversy and the obvious candidate succeeded in each instance. But the election of Archbishop Goodhew in 1993 certainly was a more heated affair. It was expected to be a contest between Bishops Harry Goodhew, Paul Barnett, and John Reid, with the first two the favorites. The ACL had not indicated which of these it preferred. With Robinson's constitutionally-driven and, some felt, over-scrupulous approach to the archbishop's role, there was a feeling among a rising generation of conservative evangelical leaders that a more radical approach to change was required.

For this generation, what the Anglican Church League offered was simply not enough. They were the first generation of conservative evangelicals who were no longer churchmen in the old sense. It had been the case that conservative evangelicals had been identified by their insistence on the *Book of Common Prayer* as the standard for Anglican corporate worship. The *BCP* was the safeguard against Tractarian innovations. But the rapid secularization of Australian society in the 1960s, the influence of the charismatic movement and the revolutionary, or at least anti-institutional spirit of the times meant that the younger clergy placed less and less faith in church order and governance to protect the truth and advance the gospel. They sensed that without a concerted effort to innovate, the church would certainly fail in its mission. The bishops' insistence on particular forms of service or forms of ecclesiastical garb seemed petty and massively out of touch.

The ACL was not to be the chosen engine of change. Politically, it has always been a defensive group operating to maintain rather than an active policy-making party. The unfortunately named REPA (the Reformed Evangelical Protestant Association) was designed to be a broad-based, grassroots movement for change, liberating the parishes from the burdensome yolk of diocesan structures to get on with the urgent task of preaching the gospel in a changing world. It was formed by a group of eighteen leading clergy who gave the impression of champing at the bit for change. Implicitly, they were sounding a rebuke to those in the generation above them who had (as they read it) fiddled while Rome burned. They were not intended to be a political movement like the ACL—the legal structures of the diocese were not the priority. It was meant to be a genuine movement for the reinvigoration of parish life for the purpose of evangelism.

REPA made two fatal errors. The first was that, for all the protests of its leaders that it was not a "political" movement, it sure gave the impression of being one. Choosing a severe-sounding acronym for a name communicated to the media and to the administration of the diocese that REPA (the "grim REPA?") was really about dividing the church and threatening to split the diocese. In a media appearance by one of its leading lights, Rev. Bruce Ballantine-Jones, news about REPA was confused with other church-political issues with which it really had little to do. This appeared on the front page of the *Sydney Morning Herald*. REPA sounded more aggressive than radical, and from then on it cast a shadow of fear. It could never escape this reputation. Long after it had become defunct, REPA was spoken of by those who feared it as if it was an active and powerful force. It achieved far more in the minds of its opponents than it ever did in reality.

The second mistake was that REPA lost sight of its original grand vision, and instead transformed itself into a campaign for the election of Phillip Jensen for archbishop at the 1993 election. There was enormous, almost unprecedented enthusiasm among the clergy for his candidacy.

Jensen was not a bishop or a scholar but rather a successful evangelist, pastor, and preacher. He was a clear-sighted leader and a visionary. He was also an iconoclast; and this was far too much for the lay members of synod, whose members are more often in the possession of cautious grey heads than not. With the benefit of hindsight, it is obvious that it was a strategy that was never going to succeed. But there was no "plan B."

In the event, Jensen surprised many by out-polling the more traditionalist Reid. But when he ran a clear third to Barnett and Goodhew, the REPA sting was drawn. It was unclear who the traditional ACL-aligned people would support, and their vote was divided. What had escaped notice was the way in which Goodhew seemed to appeal to the non-evangelicals and to those evangelicals who were more liberal on certain key issues such as women's ordination. Goodhew's campaign had focused on his strengths as a warm pastor and his experience as a rector and bishop. Not being a scholar was a positive advantage over the New Testament historian Barnett. Goodhew's successful candidacy represented a tactical failure for the ACL for which they spent the next decade trying to make amends.

The constituency had become politicized, too. The early 90s saw also the rise of two new synod parties—Anglicans Together and the "Blue Ticket." Anglicans Together was the party of the non-evangelicals in Sydney and it deliberately chose the issue of Anglican diversity and comprehensiveness as its mantra. The ordination of women was its major cause. The "Blue Ticket" was a party of more "open" evangelicals—a group including those who had supported Harry Goodhew in the election of 1993. Anglicans Together was never going to be a threat, and its members seemed to know it. The Blue Ticket, on the other hand, won some crucial electoral ground from the ACL in the early 1990s, displacing ACL members from standing committee places. It was this that woke the ACL from its slumbers. Under the presidency of Ballantine-Jones, then rector of St Clement's, Jannali, the ACL once more become a vibrant political force.

Since the 1950s, the diocese had grown increasingly complex and bureaucratic. The Sydney synod was now required to govern a multi-layered organization with large real estate holdings and substantial investments operating in a city of global importance. Furthermore, from the 1970s onwards the synod was being more frequently required to discuss issues of real theological and ecclesiological significance. The debates over the ordination of women that featured so prominently in the 1980s and 90s really have no precedent in synodical history. Synod was also invited to accept revisions to the *Book of Common Prayer* in 1978 and again in 1995. What this meant was that the synod was now a game played for very high stakes indeed.

Under Harry Goodhew, the ACL saw itself as the rightful party of government being forced to endure a stretch on the opposition benches. In the later part of the 1990s, it clawed back its losses on standing committee. In preparation for the election of 2001, there would not be a repeat of the past blunders. A clear candidate with broad appeal—Peter Jensen—was decided upon early. Other potential ACL-style candidates—Phillip Jensen and Glenn Davies—were not nominated so as not to split the more conservative vote. Even then, the election was not as straightforward as the ACL may have hoped.

Since the election of Archbishop Jensen, the League has lapsed into relative quietude. Partly this is because they have been able to count on a sympathetic archbishop who has led the way on mission rather than acted as a policeman restricting change. Furthermore, there has never been a sense of a more united synod. For example, the proponents of women's ordination have not been able to convince members of synod to revisit the question in a decade. Over the century in which the ACL has dominated Sydney Anglican politics, it has shifted in that time from being a party of broad evangelical consensus to being a powerhouse of conservative evangelicalism.

What of REPA? Some would argue that REPA's objectives were achieved even if REPA itself did not achieve them. Many of the REPA leaders—who at the time with styled themselves "colonels"—ascended to the positions of power and responsibility. Church planting was enabled and supported and the orders of ministry were loosened. But the promise of REPA was not merely of a change in policy and personnel—it was supposed to be a whole new method of doing the politics of the church. "Grassroots" was the word bandied about at the time. It heralded a whole new *ethos*; it wasn't promoted as the replica of the ACL but rather its revolutionary younger brother. In this regard, a fair assessment would be that REPA failed. It became a part of the system it had been set up to critique in the first place.

The Art of Godly Politics

Can church politics be played Christianly? We cannot have any truck with the holy height from which some direct their sneers at the business of church politics. Politics is just a reality of the *polis*: of the city of God as much as the city of man. Authority and power are not of themselves tainted, but given to be exercised with due judgment. As in the state, so in the church: human judgments are imperfect. Their imperfectability does not make them any less necessary. Calling the arrangement and distribution of power and authority in the church "politics" allows us to notice the humanity of the process and so to reckon with its fallibility. The most dangerous and tyrannical regimes in the church arise when the existence of politics is denied and the exercise of power is coated with pious language. The piety of "comprehensiveness" is oftentimes used in this way with worldwide Anglicanism. It gives the appearance of disinterest and balance and conceals the interests that it really serves.

There ought to be no embarrassment then at the existence of a group like the Anglican Church League. They can and have played their part in the good operation of the fellowship of churches in Sydney. They have often done the hard work of convincing people they need to be involved in diocesan affairs in order to ensure its proper, open, and effective management. Whereas in other dioceses power congeals in a mysterious way around the bishop, encouraging active participation in the political workings of the Sydney diocese aids in the distribution of power and the involvement of the laity.

Even conceding that politics is a necessity within denominational structures, it is imperative that those who engage in such a process act in such a way that the name of Jesus Christ is honored. How could this be done? I offer six principles as a beginning. First: *a godly church politics proceeds on the basis that the quality of the means matter more than the delivery of the ends*. It refuses to accept the "whatever it takes" mentality of politics in the secular sphere. This is because church politicians ought to recognize the sovereignty of *God* in practice as well as in theory. The Christian life itself is not about managing outcomes, but about conducting oneself in a manner that testifies to the God in whose hand those outcomes lie. The principles for conducting church politics can surely not differ markedly from this. This principle relates especially to a view of time. Christians understand time itself as being in God's hands, and so are not concerned when a certain decision takes decades to get right. I have heard people complain: "we've been discussing this issue since the 1970s!" To which I feel like replying: "Is that all?" The Anglo-American apologist Os Guiness writes: "Means either serve our ends or subvert our . . . ends. I often hear the little phrase, "Whatever it takes" . . . The pragmatic comes before the principled and that is always counter-productive. Principled ways of doing things are more effective in the long run. They are not only right. They are wise."[6]

Second, *sanctified Christians still sin, and so godly politics ought to pursue mutual accountability as a matter of priority*. The trouble with having a great cause is that it is too easy to imagine that the sanctity of the cause transfers onto those who share in it. The child abuse scandals in churches across the denominational divides have spread because of this naivety. But a properly biblical theology of sin recognizes that Christians still share in the weakness of the flesh. Article 19 of the *Thirty-Nine Articles* is quite clear on this: "And this infection of nature doth remain, yea, in them that are regenerated, whereby the lust of the flesh . . . is not subject to the law of God."

Proceeding on the basis that everyone ought to be answerable takes a good deal of effort and slows down the process. But people become addicted to power like they become addicted to pornography; and the consequences can be just as devastating, even when there is no malevolence of intent. In practice, this means ensuring for example that the same people aren't serving on committees at several levels of the church's administration. I would urge the synod to consider limiting the terms that people can serve on diocesan committees—including and especially the standing committee—to nine years, unless they have an *ex officio* position. Introducing new faces to the system would increase the health of the system by increasing accountability and access.

Third, *a godly church politics ought to seek the inclusion of women as well as men, and the young as well as the old*. The worldly tendency is for denominational structures to be dominated by older laymen and the predominantly male clergy who have a professional interest. The process becomes profoundly alienating to women simply by dint of their reduced numbers. And yet even evangelicals with a complementarian view of gender relations do not have a hierarchical view of Christian fellowship. By not reflecting its own diversity of membership in these

---

6. In Matzat, "The Corruption of Modern Evangelicalism," n.p.

decision-making bodies, the denomination is only operating on half its cylinder power. The response to this is not tokenism or the introduction of quotas, but rather a determination to change among those who operate with the church-political sphere.

Fourth, *a godly church politics should seek to make structures and processes accessible to those who are disadvantaged by: lack of mates, lack of legal knowledge, lack of rhetorical skill, or ethnic background.* The elaborate legal structures and procedures of the synodical process in Sydney are legendary. It may not be possible to simplify the process itself. But the unwieldy process clearly disadvantages those who have to engage with it but do not understand it. What's more, the process disadvantages those who are alienated from the clusters of friendships that have naturally developed over many years.

Fifth, *a godly church politics ought to seek to overcome the paradigm of winners and losers.* The system is set up, like most democratic and legal structures, to promote adversarialism. Synods of several hundred people can only express themselves by saying "yes" or "no," and inevitably more people will say one as opposed to the other. Christians ought to be able to see themselves and their fellowship as not governed by or framed by such a process, however. But the adversarial process produces wounds in the losers that take years to heal, if at all. It also promotes in the victors a vulgar triumphalism. Even more insidious is the tendency to demonize one's opponents. The use of military language to characterize such politics is a bad habit that ought to be broken as well—it requires the need for "enemies" and the impression that violence needs to be done to them. Granted, the NT makes use of military imagery, but usually when the enemy is the devil or when the training of a soldier is seen as an admirable model.

It needs to be remembered that for Christians the political process isn't the basis for our union—Christ is. In the end I think the remedy for this ongoing problem is that the denominational fellowship needs to find other ways to express itself—perhaps by the institution of a separate conference or event.

Sixth, *a godly church politics ought to priorities persuasion over results.* It would be possible, with sufficient numbers, simply to steamroll the synodical process with only a token amount of debate and airing of views. The difficulty for a party that is as dominant as the ACL is that it needs to take the time to keep persuading people of its views. This takes a good deal of effort, but it is the right thing to do. The ACL and other active church politicians ought to have as a priority the need to facilitate open discussion of the important issues before the synod in such a way that all synod members can have input into them. The gospel itself is a gospel of persuasion, not coercion; this ought to be reflected in the manner in which we conduct our church politics.[7]

Seventh, *a godly church politics ought to beware the temptation to use spiritual language as an instrument of coercion.* Spiritualized and quasi-pious language can be used as a means to silence dissent or to manipulate the church political process. Calling the decisions of synodical governments "Spirit-led" in effect bludgeons those who disagreed by implying that they countered the Spirit. Interestingly, it was through the Spirit in Acts 21:4 that the Tyrean disciples urged Paul not to go to Jerusalem—something he felt his divine calling had compelled him to do—which is to say, the Spirit may come down on both sides of a question! "Speaking the truth in love," from Ephesians 4:15, can become code for "if I speak what I think is the truth, however bluntly, then it will by definition be loving."

---

7. I write as a current member of the council of the ACL.

twelve

Conclusion

> I want to stake my life on the resurrection of Jesus Christ from the dead. That's the agenda; that's the news as far as I'm concerned.[1]

Evangelical Anglicans arrived with the First Fleet in 1788 and they've been asked to stand between savagery and civilization ever since. The first chaplain, Richard Johnson, could not take it for very long and returned home in some despondence. The second chaplain, Samuel Marsden, was oftentimes more magistrate than minister. Sydney's Anglicans have subsequently shared in the building of a mighty city in what appeared to all as a godforsaken corner of the world, only good for exiles and aborigines. They have felt themselves caught between their commission to preach the gospel of God's free grace to sinners and the need to decry the licentiousness, greed, and corruption upon which the new nation was being founded.

It has never been easy to peddle religion in this town. We should not overestimate the extent to which even nineteenth-century Sydney was ever a "Christian" society. There has always been a vigorously secular streak in the harbor city—exemplified by the jaunty articles in the colonial magazines *Bulletin* and *Truth*. "Wowser" is a term of contempt and derision invented in Sydney to describe those who would seek to impose their morality on everyone else, and it illustrates the kind of reaction against institutional Christianity that some Sydney-siders have considered as an identifying mark. Journalist Mike Carlton's satires of

---

1. Jensen, "Complete Transcript of Dr Peter Jensen's First Media Conference as Archbishop-Elect of Sydney."

Sydney Anglicanism

Sydney Anglicans sit in the tradition of scallywag stone-throwers against the perceived stained-glass pomposity of the city's church leaders.

Since the 1960s the tide of secularism has turned even more decisively against the churches. Speaking from the vantage point of 2012, the triumph of secularism is almost complete and is, in human terms, almost completely assured. Though Australia is by and large conservative and cautious, it is true that an argument from apparent fairness will always convince them, and that they react badly to ecclesiastical intrusion into public affairs. Middle-aged Sydney-siders, born in the mid-60s and early 70s, are by now a group of people who never even had the chance to walk away from church, since they were not taken to Sunday school and youth group by their parents. They are ignorant of the Bible and of Christian traditions and don't particularly want that state of affairs to change.

The Sydney Anglican story could read, then, as a story of decline and retreat in the face of two centuries of barely-concealed hostility. While there has been remarkable work done in the last thirty years or so, it could be interpreted as merely a rearguard action, a staving off for a generation of a collapse that must surely come. Compared to Anglicans elsewhere, of course, this halting of decline looks like roaring success. The average age of attendees in some Anglican dioceses is well over seventy years old. Never mind that: in real terms, the relative health of Sydney diocese could be read as really just a more muted failure.

Yet the vigor of the opposition has made Sydney Anglicans battle-hardened. They are toughened by bad news. They are used to ridicule. They are not shocked by invective against them. Insult them all you like; it makes little difference. You could also point to a resourcefulness of spirit and a stubborn determination to bear the gospel come what may. There is an edge to the Sydney diocese that has not yet been blunted by the relentless pressure to go quietly into what from a secularist point of view would be a sweet and silent oblivion.

It would however be a mistake for to consider this gingery determination from a merely human angle. If it is a virtue, it is so only because it stems from a faith in the rule of all things by the God who raised Jesus Christ from the dead. This must not be interpreted, by opponents or by Sydney Anglicans themselves, as a kind of divine vindication of Sydney Anglicans for their faithfulness and their commitment to doctrinal purity. On the contrary: the Anglican Church in Sydney may completely collapse and empty and be in a century's time a quirk of history, as defunct as the *Bulletin* and *Truth*. Faith in the sovereignty of God is faith that he will continue his work, not faith in the eternal security of Sydney Anglicanism.

This foundational theological belief in the sovereign rule of God in the risen Jesus Christ can be the basis for an attitude of confidence without lapsing into an ugly triumphalism or a defensive paranoia. The sovereignty of God is the basis not for a martyr complex, but for true martyrdom—which is witnessing to Jesus Christ come what may. A persecution complex is essentially self-interested and even narcissistic. A life lived for Jesus Christ, on the other hand, risks itself entirely for the good of the other without regard for self—knowing that it entrusts itself to the God who raised Jesus from the dead.

That, then, is the challenge for Sydney's evangelical Anglicans: do they put their trust in the sovereign Lord, the God of the risen Christ? The circumstances of life in twenty-first century Sydney are uncertain for those who would seek to preach Christ. The rise of the New Atheists has given unbelievers are more confident and at times strident voice. The possibility of a public sphere that more strictly polices itself against the intrusion of the religious is imminent. There is less and less native traction for the Christian message amongst those who have a churched upbringing of some kind. There is the outright fear expressed towards the religious way of being because of its association with violence and prudery.

But from the perspective of Christian faith, these difficulties are quite trivial. The job of the fellowship of churches that make up the diocese of Sydney is not to defend their own establishment or privilege. Their call, alongside other Christians, is to preach the gospel of Jesus Christ, the crucified and risen savior and entrust themselves to providence.

My argument throughout this book has been that Sydney's Anglicans have inherited a wealth of spiritual and intellectual resources that ought not to be despised by themselves or by others. Sydney's opponents are wrong to dismiss them as lightweight, un-Anglican and anti-intellectual. Sydney Anglicans ought not accept these charges against them and behave as if they are true. Advocating the cause of the gospel of Jesus Christ is certainly not going to become any easier in the Sydney of the next few decades. In order to ready themselves to meet those challenges, Sydney Anglicans need to return, with due humility, to the sources of their faith. The only recipe for security is a prayerful commitment to meet Jesus Christ as he is revealed in Scripture.

Bibliography

Adam, Peter. *Speaking God's Words: A Practical Theology of Preaching*. Leicester, UK: InterVarsity, 1996.
Baddeley, Mark. "The Trinity and Subordinationism." *Reformed Theological Review* 63/1 (April 2004): 29-42.
Barr, James. *Fundamentalism*. London: SCM, 1977.
Bebbington, D. W. *Evangelicalism in Modern Britain: A History from the 1730s to the 1980s*. London: Unwin Hyman, 1989.
Bird, Michael F., and Robert Shillaker. "The Son Really, Really Is the Son: A Response to Kevin Giles." *Trinity Journal* 30/2 (Fall 2009): 257-68.
———. "Subordination in the Trinity and Gender Roles: A Response to Recent Discussion." *Trinity Journal* 29/2 (2008): 267-83.
Birmingham, John. *Leviathan: The Unauthorised Biography of Sydney*. Sydney: Random House, 2000.
Bolt, Peter G. "The Two Reverend Messrs. Cowper: Bringing 18th Century Yorkshire Evangelicalism to 20th Century Sydney." *Journal of the Anglican Historical Society* 55/1 (April 2010): 26-37.
Bolt, Peter, Mark Thompson, and Robert Tong. *The Lord's Supper in Human Hands: Who Should Administer?* Camperdown, Aus.: Australian Church Record, 2008.
Cameron, Andrew. "How to Say Yes to the World." *Reformed Theological Review* 66/1 (April 2007): 17.
Carnell, E. J. *The Case for Orthodox Theology*. London: Marshall, Morgan and Scott, 1959.
Carnley, Peter. *Reflections in Glass: Trends and Tensions in the Contemporary Anglican Church*. Pymble, Aus.: HarperCollins, 2004.
Carson, D. A. *A Call to Spiritual Reformation: Priorities from Paul and His Prayers*. Leicester, UK: InterVarsity, 1992.
Chapman, Alastair. *Godly Ambition: John Stott and the Evangelical Movement*. Oxford: Oxford University Press, 2012.
Chapman, Raymond. *Law and Revelation: Richard Hooker and His Writings*. Canterbury Studies in Spiritual Theology. Norwich, UK: Canterbury, 2009.
Childs, B. S. *Biblical Theology in Crisis*. Philadelphia: Westminster, 1970.
Cole, Graham A. *He Who Gives Life: The Doctrine of the Holy Spirit*. Wheaton, IL: Crossway, 2007.
Doyle, Robert. "Are We Heretics? A Review of the Trinity and Subordinationism by Kevin Giles." *The Briefing* 309 (April 2004): 11-19.

Bibliography

Driscoll, Mark. *Church Leadership: Explaining the Roles of Jesus, Elders, Deacons, and Members at Mars Hill.* Mars Hill Theology Series. Seattle: Mars Hill Church, 2004.

Erickson, Millard J. *Who's Tampering with the Trinity? An Assessment of the Subordination Debate.* Grand Rapids: Kregel, 2009.

Foord, Martin. "Recent Directions in Anglican Ecclesiology." *Churchman* 115/4 (Winter 2001): 316–49.

Frame, T. R. *Anglicans in Australia.* Sydney: University of New South Wales Press, 2007.

———. *A House Divided? The Quest for Unity within Anglicanism.* Melbourne: Acorn, 2010.

Frame, T., and G. R. Treloar. *Agendas for Australian Anglicanism: Essays in Honour of Bruce Kaye.* Adelaide, Aus.: ATF Press, 2007.

France, R. T., and Alister E. McGrath. *Evangelical Anglicans: Their Role and Influence in the Church Today.* London: SPCK, 1993.

Franklin, James. *Corrupting the Youth: A History of Philosophy in Australia.* Sydney: Macleay, 2003.

Giles, Kevin. *Jesus and the Father: Modern Evangelicals Reinvent the Doctrine of the Trinity.* Grand Rapids: Zondervan, 2006.

———. *The Trinity and Subordinationism: The Doctrine of God and the Contemporary Gender Debate.* Downers Grove, IL: InterVarsity, 2002.

Goldsworthy, Graeme. *The Goldsworthy Trilogy.* Milton Keynes, UK: Paternoster, 2000.

———. *Gospel and Wisdom: Israel's Wisdom Literature in the Christian Life.* Carlisle, UK: Paternoster, 1987.

Goscinny, R., and A. Uderzo. *Asterix the Gaul.* Translated by A. Bell and D. Hockridge. London: Orion, 2004.

Grudem, Wayne A., and John Piper. *Recovering Biblical Manhood and Womanhood: A Response to Evangelical Feminism.* Wheaton, IL: Crossway, 1991.

Harris, Harriet A. *Fundamentalism and Evangelicals.* Oxford Theological Monographs. Oxford: Oxford University Press, 2008.

Hooker, Richard. *The Folger Library Edition of the Works of Richard Hooker.* Edited by W. Speed Hill. Cambridge, MA: Harvard University Press, 1977.

Jensen, M., and T. Frame. *Defining Convictions and Decisive Commitments: The 39 Articles in Contemporary Anglicanism.* Canberra, Aus.: Barton, 2010.

Jensen, Peter. "Complete Transcript of Dr. Peter Jensen's First Media Conference as Archbishop-Elect of Sydney." Online: http://www.sydneyanglicans.net/ministry/seniorclergy/archbishop_jensen/articles/45a/.

———. "Fundamentalism." Speech given at the Union Club, Bent Street, Sydney, 2002.

———. "Presidential Address." 2011 Synod of the Anglican Diocese of Sydney. Online: http://www.sds.asn.au/Site/104352.asp?a=a&ph=sy.

———. *The Revelation of God.* Contours of Christian Theology. Downers Grove, IL: InterVarsity, 2002.

———. "Theological Reflection on Lay Administration." Address to the clergy of the Anglican Diocese of Newcastle. November 11, 2004. Online: http://www.sydneyanglicans.net/archive/mindful/theological_reflection_on_lay_administration/.

Jensen, Phillip D., and Paul Grimmond. *The Archer and the Arrow: Preaching the Very Words of God.* Kingsford, Aus.: Matthias, 2010.

Judd, Stephen, and Kenneth Cable. *Sydney Anglicans: A History of the Diocese.* Sydney: Anglican Information Office, 1987.

Kaye, Bruce Norman. *A Church Without Walls: Being Anglican in Australia.* North Blackburn, Aus.: Dove, 1995.

———. "Terms of Engagement in Anglican War of Words." ABC Religion and Ethics. September 21, 2011. Online: http://www.abc.net.au/religion/articles/2011/09/21/3322886.htm.

Knox, D. Broughton. *D. Broughton Knox: Selected Works.* 3 vols. Edited by Tony Payne and Karen Beilharz. Kingsford, Aus.: Matthias, 2006.

Lawton, William James. *The Better Time to Be: Utopian Attitudes to Society among Sydney Anglicans, 1885 to 1914.* Sydney: New South Wales University Press, 1990.

Letham, Robert. *The Holy Trinity: In Scripture, History, Theology, and Worship.* Phillipsburg, NJ: P & R., 2004.

Loane, Marcus L. *Cambridge and the Evangelical Succession.* London: Lutterworth, 1952.

———. *Masters of the English Reformation.* London: Church Book Room, 1954.

———. *Oxford and the Evangelical Succession.* London: Lutterworth, 1950.

MacCulloch, Diarmaid. *Reformation: Europe's House Divided, 1490–1700.* London: Allen Lane, 2003.

———. *Thomas Cranmer: A Life.* New Haven, CT: Yale University Press, 1996.

Matzat, Don. "The Corruption of Modern Evangelicalism." *Issues Etc.* 1/1 (November 1995): n.p. Online: http://www.believersweb.org/view.cfm?ID=985.

McGillion, Chris. *The Chosen Ones: The Politics of Salvation in the Anglican Church.* Crows Nest, Aus.: Allen & Unwin, 2005.

McGrath, Alister E. *Christian Theology: An Introduction.* Oxford: Blackwell, 1994.

Myers, Benjamin. "Theologia Evangelii: Peter Jensen's Theological Method." *Churchman* 118/1 (Spring 2004): 27–45.

Noll, Mark A. *The Scandal of the Evangelical Mind.* Grand Rapids: Eerdmans, 1994.

O'Brien, Peter T. "The Church as a Heavenly and Eschatological Entity." In *The Church in the Bible and the World*, edited by D. A. Carson, 88–119. Exeter, UK: Paternoster, 1987.

Orpwood, Michael. *Chappo: For the Sake of the Gospel: John Chapman and the Department of Evangelism.* Russell Lea, Aus.: Eagleswift, 1995.

Osborn, E. F. ."Realism and Revelation." *Australian Biblical Review* 8 (1960): 29–37.

Packer, J. I. "What Did the Cross Achieve? The Logic of Penal Substitutionary Atonement." *Tyndale Bulletin* 25 (1974): 42.

Piggin, Stuart. "Address Given at the Launch of Kevin Giles' Book." Sydney, 2006.

———. "Billy Graham in Australia, 1959: Was It Revival?" North Ryde, Aus.: Centre for the Study of Australian Christianity, 1989.

Porter, Muriel. *The New Puritans: The Rise of Fundamentalism in the Anglican Church.* Melbourne: Melbourne University Press, 2006.

———. *Sydney Anglicans and the Threat to World Anglicanism: The Sydney Experiment.* Ashgate Contemporary Ecclesiology. Farnham, UK: Ashgate, 2011.

Rekers, George Alan. "Psychological Foundations for Rearing Masculine Boys and Feminine Girls." In *Recovering Biblical Manhood and Womanhood: A Response to Evangelical Feminism*, edited by John Piper and Wayne A. Grudem, 294–311. Wheaton, IL: Crossway, 1991.

Retief, Frank. "Church of England in South Africa. Testimony Before the Truth and Reconciliation Commission, East London, 17 November 1999." Online: http://web.uct.ac.za/depts/ricsa/commiss/trc/cesa_sub.htm.

Bibliography

Richardson, John. "Review: Muriel Porter, Sydney Anglicans and the Threat to World Anglicanism." The Ugley Vicar, September 16, 2011. Online: http://ugleyvicar.blogspot.com/2011/09/review-muriel-porter-sydney-anglicans.html.

Robinson, D. W. B. "The Biblical Concept of Fellowship." In *Explorations 2: Church, Worship and the Local Congregation*, edited by B. G. Webb, 79–80. Sydney: Lancer, 1987.

———. "The Doctrine of the Church and Its Implications for Evangelism." *Interchange* 15 (1974): 156–62.

———. *Donald Robinson: Selected Works*. Edited by Peter G. Bolt and Mark D. Thompson. 2 vols. Camperdown, Aus.: Australian Church Record, 2008.

———. *Faith's Framework: The Structure of New Testament Theology*. Exeter, UK: Paternoster, 1985.

———. "Origins and Unresolved Tensions." In *Interpreting God's Plan*, edited by R. J. Gibson, 1–17. Carlisle, UK: Paternoster, 1997.

Ryle, J. C. *Holiness*. London: James Clarke, 1952.

Schleiermacher, Friedrich. *The Christian Faith*. Edited by H. R. Mackintosh and James Stuart Stewart. Translated by H. R. Mackintosh, et al. Edinburgh: T & T Clark, 1999.

Southern, Humphrey. "Anglicanism Sydney Style." *Theology* 107/836 (March/April 2004): 117–24.

Storkey, Elaine. "Evangelical Theology and Gender." In *The Cambridge Companion to Evangelical Theology*, edited by Timothy Larsen and Daniel J. Treier, 161–76. Cambridge: Cambridge University Press, 2007.

Stott, John R. W. *I Believe in Preaching*. London: Hodder & Stoughton, 1982.

Taylor, Nicholas. *Lay Presidency at the Eucharist: An Anglican Approach*. London: Mowbray, 2009.

Torrance, Thomas F. *The Trinitarian Faith: The Evangelical Theology of the Ancient Catholic Church*. Edinburgh: T & T Clark, 1995.

Turnbull, R. D. *Anglican and Evangelical?* London: Continuum, 2007.

Underwood, Ben. "Preaching the Word." In *Donald Robinson: Selected Works*. Vol 3, *Appreciation*, edited by Peter G. Bolt and Mark D. Thompson. Camperdown, Aus.: Australian Church Record, 2008.

Vanhoozer, Kevin J. *The Drama of Doctrine: A Canonical-Linguistic Approach to Christian Theology*. 1st ed. Louisville, KY: Westminster John Knox, 2005.

———. *Is There a Meaning in This Text? The Bible, the Reader, and the Morality of Literary Knowledge*. Leicester, UK: Apollos, 1998.

Vanhoozer, Kevin J., Daniel J. Treier, and N. T. Wright. *Theological Interpretation of the New Testament: A Book-by-Book Survey*. London: SPCK, 2008.

Volf, Miroslav. *After Our Likeness: The Church as the Image of the Trinity*. Grand Rapids: Eerdmans, 1998.

———. *Exclusion and Embrace: A Theological Exploration of Identity, Otherness, and Reconciliation*. Nashville: Abingdon, 1996.

Wolterstorff, Nicholas. *Divine Discourse: Philosophical Reflections on the Claim that God Speaks*. Wilde Lectures. Cambridge: Cambridge University Press, 1995.

Wright, N. T. *The Climax of the Covenant: Christ and the Law in Pauline Theology*. Edinburgh: T & T Clark, 1991.

Index

A

Adam, Peter, 52, 58, 66–68
Anglican Church League (ACL), 160–172
    Archbishops and, 164–172
    Rise of, 161–164
Anglicans, 90–108
    Evangelicals and, 99–103
Anglicanism,
    Anglo-Catholic, 2, 21, 25, 32, 76, 92, 97, 113, 128, 144–145, 149, 152, 154, 162
    Evangelical, 2, 3, 7, 15, 46, 75, 76, 77–91, 95–103, 104, 106, 114, 117, 128, 149, 150, 173, 175
    Liberal-Catholic, 2, 3
    Protestant, 91–97, 98, 101
Archbishop, 22, 154, 165, 168
    Anglican Church League and, 164–172
    Canterbury
        Beckett, Thomas, 92
        Cranmer, Thomas, 92
        Temple, William, 29
    Perth
        Carnley, Peter, 22, 44, 49, 131, 134, 144
    Sydney, 165
        Goodhew, Harry, 131, 146, 147, 165
        Loane, Marcus, 97, 165
        Jensen, 28, 82, 121, 124, 153, 155, 168
        Mowll, 164, 165
        Robinson, 15, 31, 145, 165
Arianism, 47–48, 131–135

Authority, 141–143
    Men, 129–130, 131, 132, 134, 136, 140, 141–143,
    Scripture, 3, 13–18, 20, 21, 24, 26–29, 32, 33, 51, 57, 58, 91, 92, 94, 96, 97, 101, 106, 124, 127, 164

B

Barnett, Paul, 165, 167
Barr, James, 16, 18, 35–36, 52, 78
Barth, Karl, 34, 39
Bebbington, David, 100
Biblical Theology, 30–42, 61–62, 64, 78, 118, 121, 170
    Goldsworthy (Graeme) and Gospel and Kingdom, 36–40
    Moore College, 30–36, 38, 40, 42, 78
    Robinson (Donald) and, 31–36, 121
Book of Common Prayer, 93, 94, 98, 102, 103, 145, 148, 150, 151, 152, 165, 168

C

Calvin, John, 14, 27, 30, 37, 52, 58, 96
    Calvinist, 19, 26, 39, 61, 96, 101, 102
Carnell, E.J., 15, 16, 28
Carnley, Peter, 22, 44–49, 51, 54, 131, 134, 144
    Mystery and, 44–49
Carson, Don, 64
Childs, Brevard, 35, 36, 40
Church

Index

Church Of England, 5, 76, 77, 89, 91, 93–95, 97–99, 102, 103, 104, 105, 120, 149, 153, 161, 162, 163, 164
   Evangelicals and, 75–77
   Knox-Robinson doctrine of, 75–89, 114
   Leadership, 127–131
   Politics, 160–172
   Puritans and Church of England, 97–99
   World and, 109–125
Communion
   See Lord's Supper
Complementarian, 22, 137, 138, 139, 140, 141, 142, 170
Complementarianism, 135, 136, 138, 140, 141
Connecto9, 121–125
Cranmer, Thomas, 92–94, 97, 153–154
Creationism, 14, 16

D

Divorce, 22–23, 116, 133,
Dodd, C. H., 31–32

E

Ecclesiology, 75–89, 101, 102, 114, 124, 158, 168
England, Church of, 5, 76, 77, 89, 91, 93–95, 97–99, 102, 103, 104, 105, 120, 149, 153, 161, 162, 163, 164
   Puritans and Church of England, 97–99
Eschatology, 86, 88, 113–114, 115, 118, 119
   Pre-millennial, 14, 16, 114, 113, 119
Eucharist, 93, 94, 128, 148, 150, 152, 163
   See Lord's Supper
Evangelical(s), 5, 7, 8, 15–18, 22, 25, 26, 31–33, 39, 43, 44, 46, 47, 52, 55, 58, 63–67, 79, 89, 91, 103–106, 112–113, 118, 120, 137, 141, 145, 148–149, 152–153, 157, 163–164, 165, 167–168
Anglicans, 1, 2–3, 5, 7, 8, 15, 46, 62, 91, 99, 101, 102, 103–106, 117, 149, 150, 152, 157, 173, 175
   Anglicans and, 99–103
   British, 15, 16
   Church and, 75–77
Expository preaching (sermon), 57, 58–62, 63–65
   Stott (John) and expository sermon, 59–62

F

Fundamentalist(ism), 3, 6, 7, 13–29, 34–35, 97
   Sydney Anglicans and, 13–39

G

Gender, 126
   Different roles and, 133, 136–141, 141–143
   See also Complementarian
Giles, Kevin, 131–135
   Giles controversy, 131–135
Goldsworthy, Graeme, 30, 31, 36–40, 41, 114
   Gospel and Kingdom, 36–40
Goodhew, Harry, 131, 146, 147, 165, 167, 168
Graham, Billy, 115–117, 121, 122

H

Headship, male, 129–130, 131, 132, 134, 136, 140, 141–143
Hebert, Gabriel, 32–34, 40
Hermeneutics, 38–39
Holy Communion
   See Lord's Supper
Hooker, Richard, 95, 96

J

Jensen, Peter, 18, 20, 22, 27, 53–54, 82, 121, 124, 153, 154 155, 168
Jensen, Philip, 59, 62, 63, 64–65, 68, 117, 166–167
    University ministry, 64, 117–118

K

Kant, Immanuel, 25, 48
Knox, Broughton, 32, 43–44, 49–54, 55, 61, 114, 119–120, 129–130, 132
    Knox-Robinson doctrine of church, 75–89, 114
    Revelation and, 49–54

L

Lay presidency/administration of Lord's Supper, 2, 8, 93, 144–159
    History of, 145–148
    Reasons against, 156–159
    Reasons for, 148–151
    Taylor (Nicholas) and, 152–156
Leadership,
    Gender and, 127–143
    Giles controversy, 131–135
Liberalism, 34–35, 103
Liturgy, 90–96
Loane, Marcus, 32, 97, 165
Lord's Supper
    Lay administration/presidency, 2, 8, 93, 144–159
        History of, 145–148
        Reasons against, 156–159
        Reasons for, 148–151
        Taylor (Nicholas) and lay presidency, 152–155
Luther, Martin, 14, 19, 58, 93, 94, 96

M

Mansel, H. L., 48–49
McGrath, Alister, 55, 102
Marriage, 23, 132, 134, 137, 140, 142
Men, Authority of, 129–130, 131, 132, 134, 136, 140, 141–143
Modernism/modernity, 14, 15, 16, 25, 28
Moore Theological College, 5, 6, 17, 20, 43, 49, 51, 53, 57, 58, 63, 66, 68, 97, 112, 113, 118, 120, 123, 124, 131, 142, 154
    Biblical theology, 30–36, 38, 40, 42, 78
Mystery, and Peter Carnley, 44–49

N

Newman, John Henry, 25–26, 151
New Puritans and Muriel Porter, 17–23

O

Ordination, 128, 130, 149, 153, 154. 155–156,
    Women, 2, 8, 20, 126, 130, 131–135, 136, 141, 144, 147, 154, 158, 167–168
Orthodox theology, 7, 14, 15, 22, 23, 25, 26, 35, 45, 46, 48, 52, 55, 91, 97, 134, 156
Oxford Movement, 5, 96, 99, 101, 108

P

Packer, James, 15, 46
Politics, Church and, 160–172
Porter, Muriel, 1, 2, 6, 17–23, 24, 98, 131
    New Puritans and, 17–23
Prayer, Book of Common, 93, 94, 98, 102, 103, 145, 148, 150, 151, 152, 165, 168
Preaching,
    Expository, 57, 58–59, 63–65
    Preacher as heroic figure, 62–66
    Stott (John) and, 59–62
    Word of God and, 66–67, 69–71

Index

Propositional revelation, 13, 19, 43–56
Protestant, 5, 7, 14, 19–20, 25, 26, 30, 35, 38, 62, 66, 75, 84, 91, 108, 152
    Protestant Anglicanism, 91–97, 98, 101
    Protestant Church of England Union, 163
Puritans, 58, 95, 97–99, 100, 103, 108
    Church of England and, 97–99
    Muriel Porter and the new Puritans, 17–23

R

Rationalism, 19, 21, 25–27, 100
Reformation, 17, 20, 58, 91–93, 94, 97, 133, 144, 149, 163
Reformed Evangelical Protestant Association (REPA), 166–168
Reformed Theology, 7, 17, 20, 30, 36, 39, 43, 52, 61, 65, 69, 93–94, 96, 101
Reformers, 21, 30, 37, 58, 60–61, 66, 150
Revelation, 20, 21
    Broughton Knox and, 49–54
    Progressive, 37–40
    Propositional, 13, 19, 43–56
    "Revelation in history", 35–36
    Scripture and, 43–56
Robinson, Donald, 15, 16–17, 18, 20, 24, 30, 31–36, 37, 39, 40, 49, 59, 68, 69–70, 121, 146, 165
    Biblical Theology and, 31–36, 121
    Knox–Robinson doctrine of church, 75–89, 114
Ryle, J.C., 101, 103, 104

S

Sacraments, 96, 97, 106–108, 146, 149–157
    See also Lord' Supper
Schleiermacher, 25–26
Schools, Scripture in, 109–112
Scripture
    Authority of, 3, 13–18, 20, 21, 24, 26–29, 32, 33, 51, 57, 58, 91, 92, 94, 96, 97, 101, 106, 124, 127, 164
    Clarity of, 20
    Interpretation
        Allegorical, 31, 60
        Canonical, 36, 39
        Literal or "plain reading", 18, 20, 60–61
        Literalistic, 15, 18
    Revelation and, 43–56
    Schools and, 109–112
Separatism, 19, 23
Sermon, 57–71
    Expository sermon and John Stott, 59–62,
Social justice, 23, 100, 119–121, 123–124
Special Religious Education (SRE), 109–112
Stott, John, 15, 59–62, 64, 104–105
    Expository sermon and, 59–62
Submission of women, 128–130, 137–140
Subordination(ism), 131–135
    Trinity and, 131–135
Synod, 22, 23, 82, 89, 124, 126, 128, 141, 145–147, 161–164, 167, 168, 171–172
    Anglican Church League, 161–164

T

Taylor, Nicholas, 93, 148, 152–156
    Lay presidency at the Eucharist, 152–156
Theology, Biblical
    See Biblical Theology
Thirty Nine Articles of Religion, 61, 93, 94–95, 97, 102–103, 104, 106, 107, 108, 151, 170
Trinity, 25, 106, 131–135
    Subordinationism and the Trinity, 131–135

U

University ministry, 64, 117–118

W

Warfield, B.B., 26
Wesley, John, 25, 59, 99, 100

Whitfield, George, 59, 100
Woodhouse, John, 63–64, 135
Women
    Ministry, 22, 105, 126–143, 155, 170
    Ordination of, 2, 8, 20, 126, 130, 131–135, 136, 141, 144, 147, 154, 158, 167–168
World, Church and the, 109–125

www.ingramcontent.com/pod-product-compliance
Lightning Source LLC
Chambersburg PA
CBHW070921180426
43192CB00038B/2156